From victi

Other books by this author

Children and families—an Australian perspective (1994)

Teaching personal safety skills to children with disabilities (1994)

Why my child?: Supporting the families of victims of child sexual abuse (1993)

Teaching children in the first three years of school (1990, 2nd edn 1994)

Keep children safe (1988)

Child sexual abuse—confronting the problem (1986)

From victim to offender

How child sexual abuse victims become offenders

November 1st 2014.

Edited by
Freda Briggs

John. 13:1.
HE Loved the m into the very End of His
1st Corinthians. 13:8 Life.
Love never dis-appears.
JESus displays His Unflagging
Love ... in the Cross ...
and in the act of self-abasing,
Love, the ALLEN & UNWIN foot-Washing
that anticipates the Cross.
By D. A. Carson.

Names and places have been changed where necessary to protect victims.

The study of the early childhood and family experiences of convicted child molesters and men who were sexually abused in childhood but were not offenders was funded by the Australian Criminology Research Council. The views expressed in this book are not the views of the CRC.

First published 1995
Allen & Unwin Pty Ltd
9 Atchison Street, St Leonards, NSW 2065 Australia

National Library of Australia
Cataloguing-in-Publication entry:

From victim to offender. How child sexual abuse victims become offenders.

ISBN   1 86373 759 6.

1. Child sexual abuse. 2. Adult child sexual abuse victims.
3. Child molesters. 4. Sex offenders. I. Briggs, Freda.

362.764

Set in Garamond 10/11.5 pt by DOCUPRO, NSW
Printed by SRM Production Services Sdn Bhd, Malaysia

10 9 8 7 6 5 4 3 2 1

Contents

Preface

What do offenders see as the cause of their offending? What rewards do they get from offending? And what use is such information? Quite simply, we have little chance of changing an offender's behaviour unless we know more about that behaviour and what causes it. Offenders often see the causes of their offending quite differently from how other people see them. Unless we can understand behaviour from the offender's perspective, we run the risk of targeting them with inappropriate programmes and therapy which will do little to address the real causes of their offending. The causes they give for offending or the way they perceive their behaviour may seem totally irrational or unacceptable to us but it is the reality of their world. Only by seeing it through their eyes can we understand what motivates their behaviour to help them change.

> Dr Meryl McKay, Department of Justice, New Zealand, 1993

In 1992, a study was undertaken which involved the investigation of the early childhood and family experiences of male prisoners who had been convicted of offences against persons (as distinct from offences involving property). Although all of the men declared that they had not been sexually abused in childhood, when they were asked about their early 'sexual experiences', all but one of the convicted child molesters revealed that they had suffered prolonged sexual abuse at the hands of several different adult offenders but that they had not defined that behaviour as abuse for a variety of reasons. And although, when we interviewed them, all of the convicted child molesters were about to be released on parole and some had also served previous prison sentences for similar offences (which they freely admitted), none had been involved in any sex offender programme to address their behavioural and attitudinal problems. Given that they regarded their early sexualisation as 'normal' and were unaware of its damaging influence on their lives, none of the men had sought counselling relating to their childhood experiences. And while all admitted being sexually attracted to children, they either blamed their victims or denied the offences for which they were currently in prison.

Because child sex offenders are despised by the rest of the prison population, all of the interviewed men had experienced violence at the hands of other inmates. They viewed their survival in jail as being dependent on concealing the nature of their offences, isolating themselves and 'keeping a low profile'.

All but one of the prisoners were early school leavers who had experienced emotional and physical abuse in large, affectionless, impoverished families or foster homes. Those who lived in two parent families had either absent or non-functioning, brutal fathers, most of whom were alcoholics. And all of the men had histories of chronic ill health, unemployment and unsatisfactory sexual and social adult relationships.

A survey of newspaper reports showed that, while professional, middle-class men were convicted of similar offences, in South Australia they were much more likely to receive a good behaviour bond than a prison sentence. In 1993, with the assistance of the Australian Criminology Research Council and departments responsible for correctional services, the study was extended to include 84 child sex offenders in other prisons and other States. Their childhood histories were then compared with those of men who were sexually abused in childhood but who had not committed offences against children. Altogether, two hundred men were interviewed.

It was recognised that the researchers were entirely dependent on the honesty of this group of 'non-offenders'. It is to their great credit that they provided very frank information relating to the ways in which their abuse had damaged their sexual development, their capacity to engage in trusting adult relationships and had influenced their tendency to view boys in particular as being 'sexually attractive'. Twenty-one men were removed from the 'non-offender' group following admissions that they had sexually molested younger boys during childhood and adolescence. Most of these offences had been instigated by male adult caregivers. Most respondents viewed their childhood family relationships as affectionless; none of the offences were reported and most victims assumed that they were victimised because they were obviously homosexual, albeit at five or six years of age.

Listening to these abuse survivors, it became clear that the strongest deterrent to the commission of offences with children was their sensitivity to the damaging effects of abuse on their own lives and their reluctance to inflict the same curse on other human beings.

None of the men in the 'non-offender' group had married. Regardless of age, they had no interest in and little experience of sexual relationships with women and although some had joined the 'gay' community, this decision was not taken lightly and involved a great deal of counselling. The majority of abuse survivors felt that they were in a sexual void.

Although 38 per cent of the subjects in the study had been victimised by older females, 100 per cent were abused by men. It appears that their early sexualisation was recognised by deviant adults and they were all re-abused by other offenders. The only boys who realised that what was happening was wrong and reported it were those who were subjected to sadistic forms of sexual abuse in boarding institutions: they were either punished or re-abused for disclosing the offences.

At this stage, men in the non-offender category were the ones who responded to advertisements in the newsletters of organisations catering for male interests. They differed from the prison residents in that they were all articulate, well-educated professionals. It is also significant to note that they had all been involved in counselling programmes to deal with depression, suicide attempts or relationship problems and most had disclosed their abuse for the first time during these sessions. Most of the men had long histories of ill health, career change and deferral, and changing and failing university courses. Several had taken up to ten years to gain their first degree.

Other appeals for help were published in university newsletters and a radio broadcast. They produced responses from men who felt that they had suffered no long-term damage from their abuse. Although most of the men had experienced several abusive experiences and more than one abuser, they attributed their comparatively trouble free survival to the fact that:

- their offenders were strangers or people of no special significance;
- they 'got away' from the abuser and felt 'in control' of the situation;
- the offences were 'one off' events involving behaviour which

would be classed as the least serious on a continuum with genital touching at one end and violent sadistic rape at the other;
- they recognised that the behaviour was 'wrong' and that the offender was the one with the problem.

In other words, these boys survived well because:

- they recognised and escaped from the abuse;
- they did not think that they had been targeted for any special reason;
- they blamed the offender entirely for what happened;
- they carried no guilt or self-recrimination into adulthood.

As a result, they were able to maintain normal adult sexual relationships.

At this point, it became apparent that, although there were similarities in the backgrounds of prisoners and non-prisoners in terms of absent or affectionless fathers and frequent changes of home and school, the differences in socio-economic and educational backgrounds were so disparate as to make the study unreliable. With research assistant Mary Williams, I accepted the invitation to visit Cooma Correctional Centre in New South Wales which housed one hundred and forty men, the majority of whom had been found guilty of sex offences. The difference between this and the previous (South Australian) prisoner group was that the men came from a wide range of professional, educational and social backgrounds, most had pleaded guilty and admitted responsibility for their offences and all were involved in an assessment and education programme which gave them new insights into their behaviour. They had ready access to a social worker and a part-time psychologist, both of whom had a long history of involvement in the programme and were highly respected by their clients.

Fifty per cent of the prisoners volunteered to participate in the study. The researchers were surprised by the openness with which prisoners revealed their own, often horrendous, childhood experiences and their own offences. This was in marked contrast to the responses of men in South Australian prisons where there was no similar programme available. Many of the men at Cooma disclosed offences which had not been the subject of complaint. This honesty was all the more remarkable given that child sexual abuse has the reputation of being the world's most consistently denied offence.

Neil was the first volunteer to be interviewed. We learned that he invited police to arrest him because he recognised the damage that he was doing to a boy. With no hint of self-pity, Neil was able to contribute clear and valuable insights into how his own child-hood abuse had damaged his social and sexual development and how and why, at an early age, he had made the transition from victim to offender. Neil had given considerable thought to the inadequacies of current child protection programmes as they relate to boys and, in an attempt to draw attention to some of the deficiencies, he disclosed his own seduction strategies in a TV documentary. Not surprisingly, this caught the attention of produc-ers of the more sensationalist television programmes and when I met him, he was debating whether or not this was the best medium for getting his message across to parents, teachers and child pro-tection services. I suggested that, if he wanted to maintain control of his message, he should put pen to paper and aim for a printed publication. Neil protested that he had 'never written more than a letter' in his life but, one week later, he forwarded the first draft of his chapter.

Shortly afterwards, I learned that there were men in prison and community sex offender treatment programmes in Western Australia who were willing to participate in the study. The author of the third chapter is one of more than 300 men who have recently found the courage to disclose that they were sexually abused in religious schools in Western Australia. He had already written his autobiog-raphy as part of his therapeutic programme and he was prepared to share this with readers.

John's chapter is the longest because it covers sixteen years of abuse by men employed by New South Wales child welfare author-ities. John was also an early school leaver with no history of writing. It was an extremely painful process for him to delve back into the first nineteen years of his life; memories that he had tried to put behind him.

Jim is not a prisoner but freely admits that 'There but for the grace of God go I'. Jim scribbled some sixty pages of hatred for his parents before he settled down to writing his autobiography.

James' views have been included in the book because, whereas Neil, John and David accepted full responsibility for their offences, James remained convinced that, despite receiving a long prison sentence in his early twenties, his own abuse 'did me no harm . . . and I did no harm'. James shows how he learned and adopted his abusers' seduction techniques and reproduced them with his own victims.

The author of Chapter 9, 'One law for the rich and another for the rest of us', explains why sex offenders in Australian prisons tend to be the less affluent, uneducated and least powerful members of the community who, unlike his father, are not protected by those responsible for law and order. During our research, we encountered several very young prisoners who, in childhood and early adolescence, were trapped in paedophile prostitution rings controlled by police officers. Without payment, the boys provided prostitution services for lawyers, magistrates, politicians and others responsible for law and order. Although these prisoners contributed to the study, they feared for their lives and were unable to disclose any information which might lead to their identification or the identification of their former clients and controllers. The chapter by a former prostitute explains his own entrapment.

Although female offenders are less common than males, we felt that it was important to show that female victims may also become abusers as more than one-third of the subjects were abused by women (and this statistic also appeared in the findings of a 1993 Western Australian male survivor phone-in). The first contributor withdrew because she decided that her autobiography would fill a whole book rather than one chapter. While other women volunteers admitted that they fell into the abuser category, lacking professional support, they confined their writing to their own victimisation, finding their abusive behaviour too embarrassing and too painful to discuss. Chapter 7, 'The greatest taboo of all', explains why, because abuse by females is not acknowledged, it is difficult for victims and perpetrators to find help. Interestingly, male writers who had been sexually abused by their mothers were also unable to complete their chapters because of the ambivalence and trauma involved. Our research shows that the gender of the initial abuser determines the gender of later victims: with few exceptions, boys abused by male perpetrators went on to abuse boys; boys abused by women committed offences against women; and offenders who had been abused by both males and females victimised children of both sexes.

The first chapter has been contributed by Kevin M. Wallis, a psychologist who has worked with male sex offenders in New South Wales for the last decade.

The contributors to the study dispensed with some of the widespread beliefs about child molesters. Ninety-three per cent of the convicted child molesters had been sexually abused in childhood. The only men who had not been abused were those convicted of offences against adolescents who were slightly below the age of consent. Variables differentiating prisoners and non-offenders included a significantly higher rate of sexual abuse by females

(50 per cent) and a greater number who offended over a prolonged period of time. Prisoners (88 per cent) were more likely than non-offenders (69 per cent) to have thought that abuse was 'normal' in the early stages and prisoners (69 per cent) were also more likely than non-offenders (17 per cent) to report that they liked some aspects of the abuse. Dislike increased when boys were expected to reciprocate oral sex or submit to anal sex. Many were involved in what they perceived to be caring relationships with paedophiles and when these were the only demonstrably affectionate relationships in their lives, they tolerated painful sex for the sake of the relationship.

It is possible to see what constitutes sexual abuse being construed positively by some young, uninformed, affection-starved victims. This factor may be important to remember when trying to understand the replication of abuse across generations (Briggs, Hawkins and Williams, 1994).

We found that many of the prisoners had long been dissatisfied with their lives and desperately wanted to change. Some had tried to find help but, because of the lack of a rational societal approach to the problem and the fact that support services for offenders are scarce and not well advertised, they were exposed to often damaging intervention by inexperienced counsellors and church workers eager to gain new converts. Again and again, these men were assured that if they confessed their sins and repented, God would provide a cure. When confession failed to change their sexual preference, they were discouraged from seeking help from child protection authorities because of the belief that in States which have mandatory reporting, counsellors would be legally obliged to report them to police. Defence lawyers also deterred clients from pleading guilty to offences involving children. They were told that judges often mete out severe punishments to those who save their victims from the ordeal of telling their story in court by accepting responsibility for their crimes. On the other hand, legal advisers often made it clear that if the men pleaded 'not guilty', it would be relatively easy to confuse and discredit their child victims in the witness box, providing a high chance of acquittal.

Child molestation is one of the most hated crimes in the criminal system. Where there are no special facilities, offenders are often treated violently by granny rapists, murderers, bank robbers and other prisoners who believe that they have the right to deliver such punishment. Many people in the community take comfort from the thought that there is rough 'justice' within the prison system and child molesters get what they deserve. Others demand that judges 'lock the bastards away and throw away the key'. The reality is that most child sexual abusers are not reported; they escape prosecution if their victims are young or lack the sophisticated communication skills necessary to withstand questioning by lawyers in adult criminal courts. As a result, only about one per cent of reported offenders receive prison sentences and, with remission for good behaviour, their sentences are comparatively short.

So, although child sexual assault is a very common problem, the vast majority of child molesters are not in prison; they are in the community. Furthermore, as we found in South Australia, when prisons lack special facilities and a rehabilitation approach for child sexual offenders, perpetrators are unlikely to accept responsibility for their offences if there is a danger that they will be identified and subjected to violence by other inmates. Finally, history shows that imprisonment does not, by itself, change men's attitudes to children nor does it change their sexual orientation. International and Western Australian statistics suggest that, without intervention, 80 per cent of incarcerated child molesters re-offend within one year of their release—and they are only the ones we know about!

Common sense tells us that, if offenders were damaged by abuse in childhood, there is a tremendous amount of work to be done to create self-awareness and changes to attitudes and behaviour. If imprisonment has rehabilitation as its purpose, assessment and re-education should begin on the first day of serving a sentence—if not before.

This book helps to explain the incomprehensible: how victims become offenders and repeat the behaviour which they may have hated while they were in the victim role. Unfortunately, these tragic childhood histories are not unusual; we heard similar stories throughout the two year study and were left in no doubt that the sexual violation of boys is far more widespread than reports suggest. This is not a book for the squeamish; it has been written with a great deal of courage, effort and pain by people who were victimised in the past and who hope that their stories will result in more appropriate child protection education and better services for victims and offenders in the future.

Freda Briggs
October 1994

1

Perspectives on child molesters

Kevin M. Wallis

A prominent morning radio personality recently proclaimed (in answer to a comment from a caller) that all child sexual offenders should be put away for the 'term of their unnatural lives'. Perhaps this short statement sums up the community feeling about this category of criminal. While the sexual abuse of children *is* unnatural, there is often nothing unnatural about the perpetrators. Those who believe that sex offenders are easily distinguished from non-offenders make a grave error. Until offences are revealed, most child sexual offenders are perceived by other adults as 'good blokes' or men who 'get along well with kids'. It is this social visage of normalcy that helps offenders to gain access to victims and prevents those who receive children's disclosures from believing them and taking the necessary action to stop the offences.

As child molesters are defined by their crime, it is useful, in lay terms, to define what constitutes the sexual assault of a child. The offence of child sexual assault is where an adult or someone in a position of trust or power uses that position to emotionally manipulate, coerce through threat or inducement, or use physical force to involve the child in sexual activity.

Offences range from exhibitionism and other forms of sexual provocation or suggestive sexual behaviour through to genital fondling, oral sexual acts, anal or vaginal penetration of the victim's body by any part of the offender's body, or any object used by the offender.

The following chapters of this book, written by childhood victims and adult sex offenders, give the reader a glimpse into the

1

secret domain of child sexual abuse. However it is only a glimpse because these people represent only a small proportion of those who either have been or who are still involved in the sexual abuse of children. Most of the offenders who wrote the chapters have a paedophile or a fixated sexual preference for children. Those who do not have a primary sexual preference for children are under-represented, as are the offenders who sexually assault females.

The sexual offender is usually a male who is known to the victim. Usually he is part of the immediate or extended family of the victim, a male family friend or an adult met through the victim's peer associations. Most offenders would be seen as conventional, protective and good family men with stable work histories.

This Mr Average image is not the public perception of the child molester. The public image is a stereotyped caricature of deviance— 'the dirty old man' or 'the beanie, tracksuit and runners' type of criminal, seen in television crime detection programmes. The stereotype is typically a stranger who entices children into public toilets or into his car for the purposes of sexual gratification. Although some offenders fit the description, this group constitutes a very small minority.

Other common myths about offenders are that they are mentally ill, that the offences are caused by negligent wives and their own dysfunctional, socially disadvantaged, low-income families. The reality is that the overwhelming majority of offenders have no psychiatric illness and to argue that sexual offences are symptoms of some diagnostic category only provides them with an excuse to minimise their responsibility for their own behaviour.

To describe sexual assault as a symptom of a dysfunctional family again minimises the responsibility of the offender by distributing the blame for the offence onto his wife, other family members or even the child victim.

Finally, as three of the authors confirm, child sexual assault is not confined to low-income families, but occurs throughout all classes of society.

Various estimates as to the incidence of sexual assault postulate that one in three females and slightly fewer males will be sexually molested before they reach eighteen years of age. The estimates of abuse incidence and the dramatic increase in the reporting of sexual assault suggest that child abuse is widespread throughout the community and it is illogical to place the blame on a small subgroup of fixated offenders.

The non-fixated or regressed sex offenders are those who have an age appropriate sexual preference but, at times of stress, look to children to satisfy their emotional needs (Sgroi, 1982). The role of stress is viewed as a precipitator which triggers the offence. However, while increased stress levels might be correlated with the pre-offence emotional state of the offender, there is nothing in the nature of that relationship that explains causality, that is, why an offender specifically decides to molest a child rather than choose some other stress reduction strategy.

Although sexual offences do not fit a common assumption about the motivation underscoring the crime, one postulate is that sexual offences, although sexual in character, are motivated by the psychological needs of the offender. Hence one line of studying the child molester is to examine the qualities of pre-offence stressors, and how those stressors interact with the offender's personality. Sgroi describes offender traits as being clustered about feelings of insecurity and over-dependency; tendencies to isolate from social contacts; and a coping strategy of looking to their families to satisfy all their emotional needs. Findings from a broad range of personality tests have generally been unsuccessful in identifying a personality type or traits that are common to child molesters. While some offenders may exhibit certain personality characteristics or clusters of personality traits, these findings do not establish a causative link between personality type and offence behaviour.

An issue relating to the psychological profiling of offenders is the timing of the test administration. Obviously, offenders are tested after their offences and the test results rest on an assumption that the post-offence personality profile is not significantly different from the child molester's pre-offence or pre-disclosure personality profile. Attitudinal scales might remain unaffected, however scores from scales measuring emotional dimensions (for example, depression and anxiety scores) could be significantly different given that the social and legal consequences for sexual offences are severe.

In conclusion, the question of a predisposing personality type is of some relevance but it is only one factor amid other social and situational influences.

A social perspective regarding sexual offences against children has only emerged through the efforts of feminist writers and researchers. The credit for bringing the issue of sexual assault to public attention and lobbying for the establishment of agencies to address the plight of those who have been sexually abused, belongs to the feminists.

Feminists generally adopt a socio-cultural model of sexual assault, arguing that society invests the male gender with power, while disempowering women and children. Sexual assault is perceived as the abuse of power rather than a sexual act. Herman and Hirschman (1981) contend that sexual abuse, especially the abuse of children, is a consequence of patriarchy.

> The sexual abuse of children is as old as patriarchy itself . . . As long as fathers dominate their families, they will have the power to make sexual use of their children. Most fathers will choose not to exercise this power; but as long as the prerogative is implicitly granted to all men, some men will use it.

The authors maintain that the issue of sexual abuse would have remained buried in the male-dominated society if it were not for the interest in the subject generated by the feminist movement.

Patriarchy is the premise on which the male-gender role behaviour is commonly based. The attitudes associated with patriarchy tend to emphasise control over emotions and control over others. That control is reinforced by role bound obligations. The traditional family stereotype is headed by the strong, benevolent father and provider who is responsible for the material welfare of his family. His wife satisfies the emotional needs of her husband and children while providing the logistic support at home to keep her husband functioning and earning in the wider society. The socio-political prominence given to the stereotypical nuclear family reinforces traditional gender role behaviour.

The concept of gender-based power is central to the feminist perspective on the aetiology of the sexual abuse of children. The feminists see that men are in powerful positions relative to females and children and that some men abuse that power to sexually abuse less powerful victims. It is axiomatic that more power is attributed to the male gender than to the female gender by Western culture. While the sexual abuse of children fits this direct abuse of power model, it is important to note that *the majority of perpetrators perceive themselves as powerless*. They see themselves as failures in the male role and failures in developing and maintaining age appropriate relationships. This results in offenders adopting a victim mentality to life. They resort to using children as substitutes for adult partners because they perceive children to be in a less powerful position than themselves.

Sex offenders are not a homogeneous group, either in their socialisation, their psychology or in the situations in which the abuse occurs. In my ten years' experience of assessing more than 800 imprisoned male sexual offenders who have abused children, the majority of non-fixated offenders (those who have a dominant age-appropriate sexual preference) seem to fit into this latter group. These men usually have a strong adherence to the traditional gender stereotypes but, because of self-doubt and over-dependency, they have no confidence in their ability to live up to their male role expectations. Their relationships are mostly symbiotic dependencies, either passive dependent in style or, in other cases, overly dominant, where the male tries to control his internal insecurities by controlling the others on whom he depends for emotional support. These men tend to sexualise their emotions and seem to discriminate good from bad relationships on the nature and frequency of the sexual activity.

These offenders are so emotionally dependent that any change in their partner's behaviour, no matter how innocuous, is perceived as a threat and this produces an emotional overreaction.

In any dependency, there is a reciprocity of need in that both partners will adopt positions relative to each other that complement each other's emotional needs. For example, an insecure man who hides his emotional fragility behind a tough exterior is complemented by the stereotypical dependent female gender role. The two reinforce the dependent pathology of each other. However, the price to pay for any dependency is a loss of autonomy and to maintain the dependency, individuals often forgo their desires and suppress their emotions so as to not threaten the equilibrium of their relationship.

If the disturbance in the dependency relationship is not resolved, or the pathological routine of the relationship is not restored, then the individuals look to have their dependency needs met by some other source—having an affair, substance abuse or work, for example. Some dependent individuals, when their security is threatened, turn to minors as a non-threatening source of physical, psychological and emotional support.

Dependent relationships seem to be the norm in Western culture where the individual, for the most part, has been encouraged by consumerism to define self-identity using social and occupational roles, material possessions and the approval of others.

The role of sexual attractiveness and sexual proficiency as part of the interpersonal attraction and relationship bonding process has been manipulated by media to the point of dominance where other aspects of emotional interplay between people have become side issues. Individuals are manipulated to adhere to gender role stereotypes, and the sexualisation of emotions is the process which underscores the manipulation.

Given the role of dependency in broad society, there are many dependent relationships that undergo stress or break up, yet it does not follow that the discord from those relationship problems causes child molestation. An overly dependent personality, a tendency to sexualise emotions and the opportunity to abuse a child do not explain why some men abuse children and others, who have similar factors in their psychological profile and environment, do not.

There is, at present no empirical data that establishes a causal link between personality or social situation and sex offences. The attempts to show the connection are confounded by the essentially nondescript nature of offenders who can come from different family, educational and socio-economic backgrounds and present diverse psychological profiles.

Another method of attempting to delineate child molesters from the 'normal' population is to examine offender types using their sexual preference and the behaviours associated with their offences. Wyre (1987) differentiates groups of child molesters by their primary sexual preference (either age appropriate or paedophile), lifestyle patterns, type of molestation, the frequency of offences and the manipulation strategies used to carry out their crimes. For example, 'fixated paedophiles' have a primary sexual preference for, and sexual arousal to, children. They prefer the company of children and have few, if any, adult friends. The most common form of seduction is to insinuate themselves into the trust of the child victim and, when possible, the trust of that child's parents or guardians. Typically, this type of offender is attracted to a child of a particular age who is perceived as being emotionally neglected or vulnerable.

Wyre described several other groups; for example, the 'inadequate paedophile' and the 'parapaedophile' using the same methodology, that is, the combination of offender and offence characteristics.

In the Sex Offender Assessment Programme at Cooma Correctional Centre, the same approach is used to describe different types of sexual offenders who have committed sexual assaults on children. In line with the literature, child molesters are first divided into fixated (primary sexual preference for children) and non-fixated (primary sexual preference for age-appropriate relationships). Then the two basic categories are further differentiated into subcategories, using the degree to which the offender identifies with the victim and the scale and direction of aggression exhibited by the offender as core criteria.

The fixated offenders are divided into four categories. The first category, corresponding to Wyre's 'inadequate paedophile', is called the transitional paedophile. These offenders, usually developmentally or socially delayed, have an age-appropriate sexual preference but lack the social skills to form age-appropriate relationships. They molest children as a non-threatening substitute for age-appropriate relationships. Usually, the sexual offence against a child is this offender's only sexual experience. The recall of that experience as a masturbatory fantasy reinforces the paedophile sexual preference.

The term 'transitional' is used to describe the process by which the offender moves from an age-appropriate sexual preference to a paedophile preference. The management of these offenders has been:

- to link them into social skills training programmes where they have the chance to form friendships with peers;
- to use strategies such as orgasmic reconditioning, where the fantasy of an under-age sexual partner is gradually replaced by an age-appropriate sexual fantasy.

The second descriptive category is termed the 'moral conflict paedophile'. This sex offender has a compulsive sexual preference for children and exhibits a history of emotional or psychiatric disturbance that stems from a conflict between his sexual preference and guilt relating to that preference. It is with this group of paedophiles that the use of antiandrogenic medication (Upjohns Depo Provera) is indicated; the medication reduces their sex drive and, in doing so, diminishes their intrapsychic conflict. The use of antiandrogenic medication is controversial. All of the men who are prescribed the medication at Cooma Correctional Centre are fully informed of the actions and major side-effects, and are only included in the Depo Provera programme on the basis of informed consent. All of the men have reported a subjective improvement in their emotional stability in response to antiandrogenic medication. It is this subjective reduction in emotional distress that motivates offenders to view Depo Provera as an effective management strategy.

The third category of fixated offender is the 'social conflict paedophile'. This offender argues that sexual activity with children is a variation of normal sexual activity, and that it is societal attitudes to adult–child sexual contact that create trauma for the adult and the child. These paedophiles typically describe themselves as lovers of children (mainly boys) and they emphatically deny that their sexual activity is in any way abusive. They differ from the moral conflict group in that they have no internal conflict about their sexual preference. They see themselves as a sexual subculture that is oppressed and maligned by a rigid and puritanical society. Like any subculture, these paedophiles seek reinforcement of their views and behaviour with children by linking up with other paedophiles. They join groups or clubs such as NAMBLA (North American Man Boy Lovers Association), not only to provide a focus for paedophilia and share information relating to their victims and sexual experiences but also to publish pro-paedophile literature and lobby on a politico-social basis for changes to the law to lower or remove the age of consent for sex. Such offenders see nothing wrong with their sexual preference or sexual behaviour and they are usually only motivated to modify their behaviour to avoid legal consequences.

The fourth category of child molester is the 'sociopathic paedophile'. This offender differs from those in the two preceding paedophile categories in that he or she does not identify with the victims. To this paedophile, the victim is objectified and is only used as a means of sexual gratification. While the moral and social conflict paedophiles have cognitive distortions that rationalise their relationships with child victims, the sociopathic paedophiles do not create fantasies to justify having sex with children. They set up opportunities for abuse with no expectations of creating lasting relationships with victims. They also use more traditional criminal methods (for example, abduction, alibis, threats) to avoid detection and conviction. While this type of offender can have an exclusive paedophile preference, many of the sociopathic paedophiles encountered in Cooma's sex offender programme have had age-appropriate sexual relationships. These offenders are essentially amoral and they take advantage of any sexual opportunity that affords them control over a victim.

The dimension of identification is a continuum. At one extreme there is total identification where the offender perceives no personal boundaries between himself and his victim. At the other extreme the offender has no identification with the victim. The moral and social conflict paedophile identifies with his victim in that there is something about the child's appearance (usually male) which reminds him of how he was at that age.

Of all the fixated offenders observed in Cooma's sex offender programme, only one was not sexually abused in childhood. The typical offender gains the trust of the child, either by mirroring the interests and age-related behaviour of the victim or by assuming a nurturing, supporting pseudoparent role. The paedophile has a pre-existing fantasy construct based on his own childhood experiences and after selecting a suitable child, he sets out to change the fantasy into reality with the victim playing the role the paedophile once played at a younger age. There is an autoerotic theme in many paedophile encounters.

Because the 'grooming' of victims by a paedophile is usually a long and complex process of winning friendship and trust, the victims are often unaware that they are being sexually abused. Much of the early sexual contact is subtle and suggestive innuendo rather than overt physical behaviour. The sexual abuse only becomes a reality when there is a congruence between the victim recognising the sexual motives of the paedophile and the paedophile being aware this recognition has occurred.

Paradoxically, the physical act of sex tends to destroy the fantasy for the paedophile. The reality of the sexual acts, with their threat of legal consequences and emotional rejection, impinges on the paedophile's fantasy life. Often, the offender then tries, through increased sexual attention and emotional manipulation, to gain the victim's compliance by indoctrinating the victim into paedophilia. In this process, the paedophile moves through a power circle and another generation of abusers and victims is created.

Paedophiles have a position of social illegitimacy, their sexual preference making them pariahs. They are unable to find emotional fulfilment in adult relationships. When they are involved with a child, they have the power of an adult, and use that power to abuse the child. However, once the victim is aware of the paedophile's motives, the power (as perceived by the paedophile) is transferred from the paedophile to the victim who, simply by reporting the sexual abuse, can destroy the paedophile's social reputation and career. To guard against being exposed, the paedophile either moves on to another victim or uses threats or attempts, through cajolement and bribery, to corrupt the child's psychosexual development. This is accomplished by manipulating the child into an emotional bind by transferring the blame for what has happened onto the child. For example, it is common for child victims to be told by their abuser that they are at fault because they were compliant, did not say 'No' and did not stop the abuse. Abusers warn them that, if they report the offences, police or welfare authorities will come and take them away and put them into 'a home for bad kids'. Many child victims are warned that 'If you tell,

I'll go to jail and it will be all your fault'. This is very effective in silencing children who had enjoyed some aspects of what they perceived to be caring and affectionate relationships.

If children are made to believe that they are partly or wholly responsible for the abuse, they are also led to believe that there is something intrinsically wrong with themselves compared to their peers who are not in abusive relationships. It is common for abused children to feel different and devalued compared with other children and many victims develop self-destructive tendencies and behaviours.

From our observations, it seems that the majority of fixated offenders assessed at Cooma Correctional Centre have a sexual preference for boys. Other authors have made similar observations using other groups of fixated offenders. Interestingly, many of these paedophiles do not see themselves as having a homosexual orientation even though their sexual acts with boys are obviously so. They are mostly indifferent to, or repulsed by, the thought of age-appropriate sex with either gender, and to these offenders terms such as homosexual or heterosexual are meaningless. The paedophile has a sexual preference for a child and the sexual attractiveness of a victim is based on the combined factors of the child's age, gender and an intangible factor of how well the victim fits into the identification fantasy of the offender. As mentioned earlier in this chapter, all but one of the paedophiles assessed in Cooma Correctional Centre have histories of childhood sexual abuse. In other words, if the paedophile population at Cooma is in any way representative of the broader paedophile population, we can say that most child molesters were sexually abused in childhood. This leads to the controversial question as to what role childhood sexual abuse has in the development of an adult sexual offender.

In addressing this issue, it must be stated that a history of childhood sexual abuse is no excuse for an individual who, as an adult, repeats the offences. However, if there was a direct relationship between victimisation and offending, all victims would become offenders and that clearly is not the case; other factors are obviously at work in determining who offends and who does not. Some survivors of abuse find themselves sexually attracted to children but do not act out their fantasies. Some maintain normal heterosexual relationships and become homophobic while others join the gay community.

Previously, the corruption of the male victim's psychosexual development was mentioned as being one possible outcome for those subjected to long-term sexual abuse by paedophiles. Perhaps, for this to occur, the victim has to cross identify with the paedophile. The child is not to blame and is not responsible for this process but the possibility that this process. could occur was one of the major cues which attracted the paedophile to the victim. Boys who have emotionally abusive, distant, disinterested or absent parents are preferred targets for paedophile identification. The paedophile, through emotional manipulation, places himself in a pseudo-father or mentor role in the boy's life and the continuation of this role is conditional upon the victim's sexual compliance. Thus sex becomes the currency for affection, approval and recognition. The victim is inducted into a closed, confused amoral relationship with the paedophile and is conditioned to become more emotionally dependent on that relationship.

Usually the relationship ends abruptly when the victim matures and is no longer wanted. Rejected, the victim is left with a distrust of all adults, an undermined morality, a knowledge that he has been abused (damaged goods syndrome) and, in addition, he has been taught to sexualise emotions. These moral, emotional and behavioural consequences of sexual abuse are also common to female victims; however, females are typically abused by a different gender while most males are abused by the same gender. Same gender sexual abuse, especially if the victim has had no stable same sex role models, can have a confusing effect on a victim's sexual identity. It may be that the compounding effects of associating adults and maturation with rejection, the confusion of sexual identity, the learned helplessness in abusive relationships with adults and the social expectation for males to assume a position of power in relationships, encourage some male sexual assault victims to remain fixed in a psychosexual field somewhere between childhood and adulthood. They, like their own abusers, develop sexual relationships with children. In those relationships they have power and control and are able to satisfy their emotional needs without the fear of abuse, rejection and failure that they associate with adult relationships. This theoretical model of transgenerational perpetuation of paedophilia is speculative and is included to prompt further thought on the topic. For example, whether or not young male victims of long-term sexual assault need specialised intervention strategies such as the inclusion of stable male models in sexual assault counselling services.

Paedophilia generally has its onset during adolescence. Unlike fixated paedophilia, the non-fixated offender's paedophile interest and behaviour has its onset during adulthood. The non-fixated sexual offender has a dominant age-appropriate sexual preference that is usually heterosexual. From a study conducted at Cooma, the personality profile of these offenders is similar to that of the fixated offenders, except in scales measuring gender role and levels of post-traumatic stress. The fixated offender sample had more post-traumatic stress and subjects adhered to the male stereotyped role more rigidly than did the non-fixated group of offenders.

As mentioned earlier, over-dependency on a spouse or significant other is a commonly found characteristic of non-fixated offenders. Usually their offences are precipitated by some form of real or imagined threat to their dependency. The victim is typically a female child onto whom the offender has transferred his dependency needs. In this regard he uses the child either as a substitute for, or to augment the relationship with, or to replace an age-appropriate partner.

The non-fixated offender is often called a regressed offender (Srgoi, 1982, p. 216) in that the offender retreats from a problematic but age-appropriate sexual relationship to seek emotional and physical fulfilment in a sexual relationship with a child. However, the term is somewhat confusing because regression creates an impression that the offender is devolving to a childlike state that corresponds to the developmental stage of the victim. Observations of this type of offender suggest that rather than regressing to childhood, they project their adult needs and expectations onto their victims with the result that the children are encouraged to forsake childhood and become pseudo adults. To avoid confusion and to posit the responsibility for offences onto the offender (rather than a process of devolvement), the non-fixated offender in Cooma's sex offender programme is labelled as a 'compensatory sex offender'. The offender compensates for relationship failure, real or imaginary, or for an inability to adjust to, or to come to terms with life-stage dilemmas, by projecting inappropriate relationship expectations onto a minor.

The compensatory offender can, like the paedophile, identify with his victim; however, it is more common for this type of offender to depersonalise the victim and for the victim to become a substitute in both reality and fantasy for the offender's preferred sexual choice. This does not mean that these offenders have lost contact with reality during their offending behaviour but, rather, that they ignore the reality of their inappropriate behaviour by manufacturing a rationale of self-centred and self-serving justifications. The main justification processes mentioned in the literature are rationalisation (for example, sexual abuse rationalised as sex education or 'I was not getting enough sex from my wife'); minimisation ('I only touched her, it wasn't really sex'); and denial ('It wasn't my fault, she sat on my knee and led me on' (albeit at the age of four)). These excuse strategies are often called defence mechanisms; however, this term is somewhat confusing in that Freud described a defence mechanism as an unconscious ego operation that protects the consciousness from unwanted intrusions from deeper levels of the unconscious. The use of the term 'defence mechanism' with regard to a sex offender could be taken by some to imply that rationalisation, minimisation and denial are unconscious processes. Such a confusion in terminology may then reinforce the 'psychologically disturbed' model as an explanation for child sexual abuse and, therefore, inadvertently provide an offender with a ready made, clinically validated, excuse.

Perhaps the starting point for a dynamic explanation of the post-offence behaviour of sex offenders is that these offenders are widely described as very poor self-reporters of their behaviour which translated from jargon to layman's language means that sex offenders tend to lie about their offences. Simply put, the compensatory sexual offender targets a child because that option is easier and less threatening than seeking emotional and physical fulfilment in an age-appropriate relationship. The abusive relationship is used either as a substitute for, or to complement, an existing relationship that is perceived by the offender to be failing or non-stimulating. Offenders use their positions of trust or adult authority to control their victims. Often, it is the exertion of that control which compensates offenders for the perceived loss of power to control their age-appropriate partners.

Although the sexual abuse of a child often occurs in a context of relationship and personal confusion, it is the result of a calculated decision by the offender who knows that what he or she is doing is wrong but does not want to admit it. A sexual offence is a crime and the first consideration should be legal intervention to stop the offending behaviour. Legal action reinforces the social reality that sexual assault is a crime and places the legal responsibility for the offences onto the perpetrator. After the offences have been notified to authorities, the offender should, in all cases, be separated from the victim, and the victim should be protected and given emotional support. The sexual abuse of a minor, especially in a family, also involves the emotional abuse of other family members. Often the discovery of the offence leaves those who are close to the offender in a state of emotional turmoil. These individuals also need help to resolve their feelings. Individual and family counselling is especially important if the offender is expected to return to the family home. A great deal of work needs to be done to change the power structure in the family, develop safety strategies for the children and, where necessary, develop the self-esteem and assertiveness of family members.

After the notification of offences, the management of those who sexually assault children has become somewhat problematic. There seems to be a growing trend to describe sexual abuse of children as a symptom of individual or relationship disturbance. This trend fuels calls for the establishment of special units and 'treatment' programmes for sexual offenders. The problem with the treatment approach is that it:

- provides the offender with a psychological rationalisation for the offence;
- creates a special case for the management of sex offenders in the criminal justice system which is not afforded to those who commit other types of crimes;
- weakens the criminality of sexual assault while strengthening the depiction of sexual assault as a syndrome or symptom; and
- is costly to establish and operate special units for sex offenders in prisons.

In the prison culture, the inmate code of ethics regards sexual offences against children as the worst type of crime. Perpetrators of such crimes are labelled 'rock spiders' by other inmates. Those who have been sentenced to prison terms for the sexual assault of children usually place themselves in protective custody. Failure to do so could result in serious assault (or worse) at the hands of other inmates. To many in the community the bashing of sex offenders in the penal system is viewed as fair retribution. However, the threatening milieu of prison only strengthens the dynamics of the sexual offence by encouraging the sexual offender to view himself as a victim, not a perpetrator, and by reinforcing the offender's use of deception and manipulation as strategies to avoid detection. Obviously, such an environment obstructs the assessment of sex offenders.

A cost-effective approach for the imprisoned sexual offender that is both humane and consistent with the legal perspective that sexual assault is a crime is to create a prison milieu within which sex offenders may be assessed without threat to their safety. At Cooma Correctional Centre, a small but very old prison in the rural south-eastern corner of New South Wales, such an environment has been created. The idea of establishing a sex offender assessment pro-gramme at Cooma was based on the assumption that the dramatic increase in the reports of sexual assaults against children would lead to an increase in the number of imprisoned perpetrators. The decision to establish a programme was based on pragmatic issues such as whether the existing buildings had the capacity to accom-modate the imprisoned sex offender population, whether the place-ment of these prisoners at Cooma was a safer, more efficient and cost-effective alternative to keeping them in protection wings of other prisons and whether sex offenders suited the industries already operating at Cooma. On the last consideration, a compara-tive study of sex offender and non-sex offender work habits was conducted and the results suggested that sex offenders would complement the existing industries of the gaol.

The next task was to neutralise the non-sex offender population's detestation for child molesters. This was accomplished by enlisting the support of other inmates to explain how the persecution of sex offenders only reinforced the criminal pathology of sex offences. More than 80 per cent of the inmate population supported the proposal and co-operated with the setting up of a sex offender assessment programme.

The strategy for the programme was based on fitting a particular type of prisoner into the existing prison system rather than creating a parallel prison system designed for a particular type of offender. Sex offenders posed special problems because, as a group, they are detested throughout the prison system. Through reasoned argument and a co-operative approach, other prisoners at Cooma assisted the establishment of an assessment programme for sex offenders. They did this because they wanted to help to protect children. A pilot project was undertaken and the small number of sex offenders in the gaol at that time attended an assessment group. From this modest beginning, which in itself proved that a sex offender pro-gramme could operate within the existing prison environment, there has been a steady increase in the number of sex offenders placed at Cooma. The Sex Offender Assessment Programme does not 'treat' sex offenders; the emphasis is on risk assessment and, where possible, risk reduction through devising offender management plans and re-education groups.

There is a role for psychological and other therapeutic interventions but only after the offender has accepted full responsibility for the offence. The measure used to assess this criterion is based on the offender's candidness about his behaviour, evidence of an understanding of the effect the assaults have had and will have on his victims and how much contrition is shown. Sex offenders as a group tend to deny, minimise and in other ways misrepresent the facts pertinent to their offences for it is the nature of the offence to be secretive, manipulative and dishonest. The verbal acceptance of responsibility by the offender cannot be, by itself, used to predict future lawful adjustment. Other variables, such as a history of violence, substance abuse, the availability of support networks, the intellectual and social capabilities of the offender, whether or not the situation in which the offence occurred has ceased to exist and the experience of the assessor must be added into the equation. As the assessment process is improved by the increased amount of information made available about the offender, the accuracy of the assessor is similarly assisted by obtaining the opinions of other professionals involved in the offender's management.

To facilitate a change in behaviour and attitude, the offenders must confront themselves and deal with their offences. During this process of taking responsibility for their behaviour and its damaging effects, the person begins to emerge. Some offenders do not want to confront their offences because their obsession with children has become so pervasive that it is an integral part of their life. They define themselves by their sexual preference for children and the pursuit of that sexual preference consumes their reality and fantasies. To give up their fixation on children would leave an unfillable emotional void. There is no solution to the problems posed by compulsive and intractible paedophiles apart from separating them from society.

By contrast, many offenders say that they were relieved when their offences came to light because they knew that what they were doing was wrong but because of fear and shame, they did not have the courage to break out of the offending cycle. To these offenders, the offence acts as a form of social suicide because, after disclosure, the offender's life is permanently changed. The task of rehabilitation is really a task of reconstruction. The offenders reflect on their past experiences and consider how these might have influenced their daily lives. The offender's past attitudes and relationships are analysed and challenged, and the offender is encouraged to salvage his life through developing new and healthier attitudes and non-abusive coping strategies.

The classification of sex offenders as described in this chapter has clinical implications with regard to specific management strategies. They might be seen as giving the offender a psychological excuse to rationalise and minimise their offences. However, this is not the case because it is pointed out to offenders that they, unlike other men in similar situations or states of despair, choose to sexually abuse children in preference to some other less harmful response to their problems. Second, by focusing on the assessment of risk, the purpose of the programme at Cooma is directed onto the protection of the community rather than onto the treatment of the offender. If the offender makes changes to his attitudes and behaviours, that reduces the risk of re-offending and both the offender and the community benefit.

As Professor Briggs mentions in the Preface, only about 2 per cent of reports of child molestation lead to official action. There is a clamour of outrage when sex offenders are identified and it may be that these few offenders are the scapegoats for society's unwillingness to address the issue of child abuse in a manner that is not contaminated by ignorance and sensationalism. Some of the individuals who have contributed to this book may have committed what are considered to be monstrous acts. However, when one works with these offenders, it becomes clear that the majority are not monsters. Unlike the rapist who substitutes violence for sex, the child molester substitutes sexual abuse for love gone wrong.

References

Herman, J.L. (with Hirschman, L.) (1981), *Father–Daughter Incest,* Harvard University Press, Cambridge (Mass.) and London

Sgroi, S.M. (1982), *Handbook of Clinical Intervention in Child Sexual Abuse,* Lexington Books, D.C. Heath and Company, Lexington (Mass.), Toronto

Wyre R. (1987), *Working with Sex Abuse: Understanding Sex Offending,* Perry Publications, Oxford

2

In search of love

For the first eight years of my life, I was a normal child living in a very ordinary working-class family in a very ordinary New South Wales coastal town. My parents were hard working, law-abiding, God-fearing people whose only ambition was to produce law-abiding, God-fearing well-adjusted children. My older brother and sister fulfilled their expectations by having happy marriages, happy families and homes of their own. At thirty five years of age, I have two criminal convictions, no partner, no children and my only home is a prison cell.

Life changed irrevocably for me back in 1965 when I was allowed to spend the long summer holiday with relatives who lived in the country. I looked forward to the holiday with a mixture of apprehension and excitement because, at the age of eight, I had never been away from home without my parents or my brother and sister. When I arrived at my destination, my relatives already had an unexpected visitor, a man named Tom who, I was told, had just separated from his wife. There was no spare bedroom in the house and Tom had already acquired possession of the sofa which converted into a double bed. I was very uneasy when my aunt announced that I would have to sleep with this middle aged stranger but, by bedtime, Tom and I were already good friends and my apprehension had eased.

Tom was different to the other adults in my life. He seemed genuinely pleased to have my company and I was flattered by his attention. He played cricket with me, kicked a ball around, talked and, more important, listened. Never before had I received the continuous attention and approval of an adult—least of all a male adult and I loved it. I quickly developed a warm, secure and rewarding relationship with Tom and when, on our first night of bedsharing, he put his arm around me and kissed me goodnight, my reaction was, 'I wish my dad did this'.

The following night, when Tom came to bed, I snuggled up to him spontaneously. On the third night, I sensed that something was different. Tom held me too tightly, his breathing was heavy and I felt something hot and hard pressing against my bare back. At age eight, I epitomised sexual innocence and had no idea what was happening.

Tom moved his hand inside my T-shirt and began to caress my body. Initially, I was surprised but not alarmed because it was a very loving touch, a touch which gave me a strange, excited feeling in the pit of my stomach. At the age of eight, I knew nothing about masturbation or what was acceptable and unacceptable in adult–child relationships. My mother had taught me to avoid dangerous strangers who kidnap children and take them away in their cars but no-one had warned me about the dangers of genital touching by people I knew and trusted.

Tom bore no resemblance to my stereotyped image of the dangerous monster who steals children. I also took it for granted that what was happening was acceptable because my aunt, a good living Christian woman, had placed us in the same bed.

Tom made me feel good about myself and I quickly grew to love him. When the holiday came to an end, I missed him dreadfully but returned home determined to have a more demonstrative relationship with my father. On the first day back, I climbed onto dad's knee and stroked his face. He pushed my hand away and told me to keep still; he wanted to watch television. So, I snuggled up close to his chest. He became irritated, pushed me aside and said, 'Don't be silly! Go away! You're big enough and old enough to sit by yourself!'

I pleaded with dad to kiss me goodnight. He told me that kisses were for 'girls and cissies' and 'boys don't do things like that'. The more I tried, the more he pushed me away. I began to wonder why Tom had found me sufficiently attractive to hug and kiss while my own dad rejected me. I reached the inevitable conclusion that my father didn't love me and Tom did. Without realising what had happened, I was already associating sexual fondling with affection and acceptance and I now wanted more.

With no adult to fondle and caress me, I turned to other boys.

My early sexualisation enabled me to share my new found knowledge and capabilities with the more curious members of my peer group. I took boys home after school and, under the house or in the privacy of my bedroom, demonstrated my new found capacity to create an erection. I convinced the boys that I could teach them how to do it and they all joined in. My mother had no idea what was happening behind closed doors. She was just happy that her son had made so many new friends who all wanted to play with him.

One day, a member of the group told me of a man who paid boys twenty dollars each for masturbating while he watched. We couldn't believe our luck that there was someone who would actually pay us for merely changing the venue of our activities. We had never owned such a large sum of money in our lives and it was impossible to resist such an offer. We went to a building site where a man was painting the windows of a new apartment block. He talked to us momentarily and invited us into the ground floor apartment which was already furnished for public inspection. We went from room to room, marvelling at the lavish furnishings until, finally, we reached the bedroom. The man told us to undress, sit on the bed and play with each other's genitals. He sat on a chair in the corner of the room and merely gave instructions. It seemed a very strange thing for a grown-up to do and I felt a bit embarrassed but I forgot the embarrassment when he paid us. This was the mid-1960s and $20 was a great deal of money for a child to receive—especially for engaging in something that we already did routinely in my bedroom at home.

A few days later, I called on my friend but he wasn't at home. It occurred to me that he might be visiting the painter at the apartment block (earning more money) and I went to look for him. He wasn't there but the painter was and he invited me into the apartment and sat me down on the bed. He asked questions about school, my family and friends. He then told me that he had something that would interest me. He left the room momentarily and returned clutching a pile of journals. He sat by me on the bed, showing me pictures of adult males who were involved in sexual activity with young boys. I had never seen anything like this before but my initial curiosity quickly turned to fear. I did not like these 'rude' pictures and said so. He assured me that it was 'only sex' and sex was for fun—everyone likes doing it, and after all, I'd already demonstrated that I enjoyed genital fondling. I suddenly felt guilty but with more persuasion about the normality of what was happening, I agreed to undress and he began to suck my penis. This was even more confusing and more exciting than my earlier experiences with Tom and I didn't resist when he rolled me over, burying my face in the pristine, luxurious bedspread. The man's demeanour suddenly changed and I panicked. I asked him what he was doing and he told me to 'shut-up and just do as you're told. You've had your fun. Now, it's my turn.'

I was terrified and yelled that I wanted to go home. He held me down and raped me. The pain was unimaginable. I felt my anal opening tear and I was convinced that the man was killing me. I screamed at him to stop but he merely pushed my face down into the bedding to deaden the sound. When it was over, the man released me and I ran into the toilet. I was in a state of shock and could not understand why someone who had befriended me and given me a good time had, only a few minutes later, tried to kill me.

In the toilet, I confirmed that I was bleeding badly and the pain was intolerable. I was very distressed and the man began to panic about his own safety. He urged me not to tell anyone about what had happened because it was really my own fault and I would get into big trouble if I 'told'. 'After all,' he said, 'you asked for it . . . You came here voluntarily. You knew what would happen.'

When I left, I tearfully assured him that I would tell no-one. I went to the park behind the local shopping centre, lay down behind a bush and wept uncontrollably. I was afraid to tell my parents about my injury because I knew that they would take me to the hospital and someone would question me about what had happened. I was worried about the damage inside my body but even more worried about the consequences if they discovered that I was responsible for this . . . that I was the bad boy who had 'asked for it'. I knew that it would be impossible to explain it as an accident. I removed my bloodstained underpants and left them in the shrubbery, recognising that I would have to cope alone . . . that no-one could help me and whatever happened, I had to stay out of trouble.

The pain during the following weeks was excruciating. I gritted my teeth when necessity forced me to use the toilet. I found it difficult to walk and just as difficult to sit on the hard chairs at school. I withdrew from everyone, unhappy, afraid of disclosure and the inevitable rejection and punishment. I lost my appetite and spent a great deal of time in my room. No-one appeared to notice that anything was wrong.

I never went back to the flats. Two years later, I learned from my aunt that Tom had moved into our neighbourhood and he wanted me to call. I went to his house after school and he was clearly happy to see me. We talked and talked and I was overjoyed to find that he still listened attentively and responded affectionately. I could talk to Tom about anything and he never silenced, belittled or reprimanded me. He answered questions about the sexual things that would have embarrassed and annoyed my father. The most rewarding conversations I had with him were those which took place in his bed while he was fondling me.

One day, Tom took me by surprise by asking if I had ever tried anal sex. I told him what had happened with the painter. This was the first time that I'd told another adult and it was a huge relief to get it off my chest. Tom assured me that the man was entirely at fault . . . the experience should have been enjoyable, not painful. He gently rolled me over, saying that he would show me what he meant. I protested strongly as memories of the pain flashed through my mind. I struggled but, again, he gave gentle reassurances that I would like what was about to happen. And when I protested that I was in pain, he assured me that it would soon pass . . . 'Just wait and see . . . you'll like it', he said. I waited and hated it but could not escape. I clasped my fists tightly as I waited to be released. When he finished, Tom rolled me over, looked down into my face, smiled and said, 'You liked that, didn't you? That was terrific'.

I was bewildered. There were tears of pain rolling down my cheeks and here was the man I loved smiling down at me, assuring me that I should have been enjoying what he did to me. He was so persuasive that I began to think that the problem was mine. Why did I find it so painful when I was supposed to be enjoying it? What was wrong with me? Why was I abnormal?

Tom assured me that it would get better with practice and he 'practised' whenever we were together.

Over time, I learned to block out the pain but I continued to hate what he did. So why did I return? I have often asked myself that question and the answer is clear. I was starved of male affection and Tom filled my emotional needs. He was the only adult who gave me the empathy, approval, attention and affection that I so badly needed. I loved his caresses and the times when he comforted me. I loved talking to him because he listened and understood. And I came to the conclusion that if anal sex was the price I had to pay for love, I was prepared to tolerate it.

By the time I was ten, I was exhibiting signs of early sexualisation which were easily recognised by other paedophiles. The men were often loitering in public toilets and, occasionally, I would be offered a substantial sum of money to let them touch my genitals. Sexual touching was now a normal part of my life. I refused the much higher sums of money offered for anal sex but some men refused to take 'No' for an answer and forcibly raped me. Whenever this happened, they reminded me that I was powerless: nobody would believe the word of a child of ten against the word of an adult . . . least of all men who were teachers, lawyers, clergy and others with professional standing. Furthermore, if I *was* believed, I would still get into serious trouble because I had voluntarily gone into the toilet cubicle and removed my clothes for sex for payment. That made me a very bad boy indeed.

My early sexualisation resulted in the premature arrival of puberty. My pubic hair was a source of wonderment to the boys in my peer group and they needed no persuasion to observe my enviable growth. I was playing under the house with another boy when my penis erupted and discharged what I thought to be a quantity of puss. This had never happened before. Despite my experiences with adults, I'd never seen anyone ejaculate and I was terrified. My only sex education was limited to what I had learned from sexual abuse and I feared that there must be a boil or an abscess inside my genitals or, worse, that I was suffering from a deadly disease. The anxiety curbed my sexual activity for several months. I was desperately worried, fearing that my parents would recognise my symptoms and take me to the doctor who would confirm to the world that I was a wicked, evil boy who seduced innocent men.

One weekend, my brother's friend came to stay and we shared the same bedroom. He introduced the topic of masturbation and I plucked up the courage to confide in him about my terrible problem. He laughed at first but went on to explain that I was normal. Any sense of relief that I experienced from this news was short-lived because he then urged me to masturbate him to enable him to demonstrate how boys and girls make love to produce babies. I was horrified to learn that boys were supposed to do this with girls, not each other. After all, men had been telling me that they loved me for the past two years and their 'love' always involved sexual touching.

At school, I gradually became the object of curiosity and cruel jokes. Others learned of my ability to ejaculate and I was constantly being asked to provide demonstrations for my disbelieving peers.

I complied with most requests because I longed for their acceptance and approval.

Far from increasing my popularity and providing friends, my performances merely earned me the label of 'poofter' which, in turn, resulted in derision and violence from older boys. I often returned home from school with torn shirts, cuts and bruises which I always explained as 'accidents' even though this resulted in nagging for being stupid and clumsy.

Once I realised that sex was meant for men and women, I was convinced that there was something wrong with me. Why did men choose me instead of women? Was I really a 'poofter'? What did it mean?

I'd already been indoctrinated by my abusers with the knowledge that, if a boy is violated by a man, it's his own fault and he's a bad boy. Boys are supposed to protect themselves. 'Be strong . . . be a man . . . stick up for yourself . . . hit him back . . . boys are brave . . . they don't cry'; these were the messages that were drummed into me by my well-intentioned parents and teachers. At ten years of age, how could I tell anyone that there was something wrong with my sexuality?

Before they reached puberty most of my friends had stopped the homosexual activities associated with normal peer group curiosity and were showing an interest in girls. I withdrew more and more into my own lonely world, convinced that I was born to be different. I could not cope with clubs or sports because the macho males had already branded me as 'gay' and someone to be taunted or avoided. When I was allowed to join a mixed group, I was always paired off with the ugliest girl or the one with a disability who was otherwise unwanted. Friendships with girls were rare and of short duration because someone always jeered at them for associating with the school 'poofter'. Once labelled, there was no escape. I hated myself for what I had become and when I was tormented at a school sports event, my control snapped. Until then, I had always been the victim who never fought back. On this occasion the years of suppressed anger surfaced and gave me unprecedented strength. I leapt on the boy, bashed his head on the ground and thumped him mercilessly. I wanted to kill him in revenge for the years of persecution and suffering. I had had enough!

It took two teachers to restrain me and drag me away from my surprised victim. The teachers were equally surprised and, to their credit, invited me to disclose what was wrong. I plucked up sufficient courage to confess that I was desperately tired of being

24

rejected, humiliated and referred to as 'poofter'. They enquired why I was given this label but I pretended that I didn't know.

I knew that homosexuals were despised by society and I hated the thought that I might be one of them. I wanted to ask my parents about why God had made me 'gay'.

I practised what I could say to them but there was never any opportunity to mention the subject. All avenues of communication were firmly closed when they declared their distaste for all aspects of homosexuality. I recall the occasion quite clearly.

We were watching a television news report to the effect that a university student had been expelled for having possession of homosexual literature in his locker. My parents were united in their confirmation that the student deserved his punishment and society did not need people who were so sick in the head. I wanted to leap up and cry out that they were damning me but I lacked the courage and went to bed, sobbing unconsolably into the early hours of the morning.

I took it for granted that I was also 'sick in the head'. Why else did men pick me out and offer me money for sex? How did they know that I was willing and had done it before? What was it about me that marked me as different from everyone else? And if everyone else could see that I was different, why couldn't my parents see it? Why didn't they question? Why did they ignore it? Was it because they, too, were ashamed of me?

The subject of homosexuality was never raised again in my presence. Sex was a taboo subject and my parents showed little affection to each other. My father had his own problems and coped by immersing himself in work. On the rare occasions that we saw him, he was grumpy and distant.

At a time when my peers were creating normal sexual relationships with girls, I spent more and more time with younger boys. They were the only people who did not reject me. Neighbours stared, pointed and gossiped about me but my mother always rose to my defence. Her motto was, 'Hear no evil, see no evil and speak no evil' and, like the three wise monkeys, she refused to see the obvious. My mother hoped that, by ignoring the problem, I might eventually 'grow out of it'. She thought that she was protecting me but, in reality, she was protecting herself from the realisation that one of her sons was, indeed, very different to the norm. She closed down every opportunity for discussion and I knew that I had to cope alone.

I left school when I was fourteen. I couldn't concentrate or take an interest in school subjects because the focus of my life was to avoid the daily verbal and physical abuse of my tormenters. I found a job at Woolworths supermarket which was close to home. The work was relatively mundane but I loved being there because, for the first time since I was eight, I was treated as a normal human being. I was respected and praised for the work that I did well and I responded gratefully.

Life progressed peacefully until one of the school bullies from my past was given a job at the store and my life became hell thereafter. He told other staff that I was a 'poofter' and the taunts returned.

I turned to alcohol to dull my senses. At lunchtime, I escaped to the nearest hotel and drank as many vodka and orange drinks as I could consume in half-an-hour. This diminished my sensitivity so that I could cope with the taunts for the rest of the afternoon. I spent more and more time and more and more money in the hotel and the more I drank, the more depressed I became.

On my sixteenth birthday, I made my first suicide attempt. On my way home from work, I found myself surrounded by a group of former school friends. At first, they pretended to want to talk to me but, gradually, they became more violent, pushing me from one person to the other, jeering in unison and, finally, punching me to the ground. They left me on the footpath, my clothing torn and covered with blood. They called out, 'We hate poofters. Poofters are scum' and ran down the street laughing. No-one came to help me and I decided, there and then, that life wasn't worth living. I found an empty bottle, broke it and slashed my wrists. Leaving a trail of blood on the footpath, I staggered home shouting 'I'm a poofter. I don't deserve to live' at the top of my voice. My parents heard the noise and came out into the street. I longed to tell them of my despair but my father was only concerned about 'what the neighbours might think' and urged me to 'calm down'.

Dad took me straight to my bedroom then, his mission completed, he turned away and closed the door. There was no conversation about my dishevelled and bloody appearance. No-one mentioned it when I emerged from my bedroom the following day. I was longing for someone to say something . . . anything . . . but they all behaved as if nothing had happened. The message I received from the silence was, 'You have a problem but we don't want to know about it'.

I realised that I would have to leave home to avoid causing my parents further embarrassment. I went to live in the local caravan park. It was terribly lonely for a boy of sixteen and I drifted from job to job, lacking motivation and self-respect. Sex was my only source of comfort and even that took a self-destructive form. Unable to relate to anyone, I toured public toilets looking for momentary company and momentary relief. Afterwards, I emerged feeling sick and despicable.

I made friends only with the younger boys in the caravan park. By now, I was seventeen and they ranged from age nine to fifteen. They were at the curious stage and I let them have use of the van in exchange for sexual favours. One of the mothers heard about what I did and she had me evicted from the park.

Humiliated, I returned home and took a job at the steelworks. My parents bought me a car for my eighteenth birthday. My only friend was then a fifteen-year-old boy who delivered the mail to my section of the factory. John lived in the next street and I gave him lifts to and from work when our shifts coincided. Sometimes, his parents allowed him to stay overnight at my house and on one such occasion, I persuaded him to engage in oral sex. I rewarded him by allowing him to drive my car to work when he was on night shift. He didn't have a licence and I knew the risk that I was taking but it was something that he enjoyed.

Spending a great deal of time with John, I soon became acquainted with his sixteen-year-old sister. Sue and I became good friends and we often went out together. She was the only girl who was willing to be seen in public with the local 'poofter' and for that I was extremely grateful. I liked Sue a lot but, looking back, I now realise that the relationship developed because it increased my access to John and deflected his mother's growing suspicions of my sexual abnormality.

I failed to pick up the clues that Sue wanted more than friendship and I was completely stunned when she proclaimed that she was in love with me. In my own way, I loved her too but it was not the kind of love that she wanted. Much as I longed to respond to her affectionate gestures, I had received no preparation for an intimate heterosexual relationship and I froze and withdrew in embarrassment. I didn't want to hurt or deceive Sue and, in the end, I pleaded with her to find someone else. I confessed that I loved her brother, not her. I even told her that John and I had made love when we slept together. This failed to deter her and by sheer persistence, she eventually found a place in my bed. For the first time in my life, I held a girl close in my arms and made love to her. I was deliriously happy and wanted to proclaim to the whole world that, after all my anxieties and all the taunts, I was normal.

My euphoria was short-lived. My mother came to waken me in the morning expecting to find me in bed with John. She often found us sleeping with our arms around each other but, if she noticed, she said nothing. On this particular morning, she discovered that I had spent the night with John's sister. Far from being pleased with this, the only evidence of my normality, my mother 'hit the roof'. She ranted and raved and informed me in no uncertain terms that sleeping with girls was sinful and banned. She and my father forbade me to see Sue again and, by contacting her parents, they ended my first and only heterosexual relationship.

This increased my dependency on John. He was less demanding, more predictable and less intimidating than his sister and I felt safe with him. But, as he grew older, he also developed an interest in girls and found excuses to avoid me. Things came to a head when, after lending him my precious car, I found him making love to a girl on the back seat. I felt betrayed and hurled a brick through the rear window. That proved to be a costly gesture and now desperately lonely, I turned to drink. That increased my confidence and loosened my tongue. I shocked the entire neighbourhood by standing outside John's house proclaiming my love for him at the top of my voice. His mother came out, scolded me like a naughty child and threatened to call the police. I returned home feeling more abnormal than ever and arrived just as my mother was answering the phone. I heard John's mother yell, 'What kind of an eighteen-year-old youth claims to be in love with a fifteen-year-old boy?'. My mother paused, looked angry but calmly replaced the telephone, went into the kitchen and made a pot of tea.

I longed to expose my hurt to her but she provided no opportunity for conversation. When my mother regained her composure, she demanded an assurance that I would 'avoid that crazy family from now on' and, of course, I agreed to comply with her wishes.

Over the years, my mother received many similar telephone calls from concerned parents but she ignored them all. If she was worried about her deviant son, she failed to show it. She asked no questions and sought no explanations. She went on living as if nothing had happened.

In 1977, I was unemployed, friendless and suffering from a bout of depressive illness. When my uncle invited me to spend a holiday with him in New Zealand, it seemed a good opportunity to get away and make a new start. He lived on a sheep station in the North

Island and I became a shepherd. Life in rural New Zealand was very lonely for a twenty-one-year-old and, after a few months, I longed for company. My prayers were answered with the arrival of a youth who came to live and work on the property. We related to each other instantly and became good friends. I soon persuaded him to share my bed which he did for eighteen months. He then left, quite suddenly and without explanation. I was devastated. I found additional work as a barman to fill the time. I'd been working there for several months when I was invited to a party by one of the staff. She was a single parent with two attractive sons, aged nine and twelve. I befriended the mother and that gave me access to the boys. They enjoyed the presence of a father figure who could take them to sports, play with them and provide the cuddles and hugs that they needed. I developed their trust by encouraging their confidences, engaging in the kinds of conversation that they could not have with their mother.

I sexually molested these boys and three others in a similar single-parent family for all of two years. During that time, I aroused no suspicion and the boys never complained. Significantly, when I was reported, it was by a girl. When I spent weekends with these families, I was expected to sleep on a portable bed in the lounge. The mothers trusted me because I made no sexual demands on them, 'got on well with the kids' and took them on outings, enabling the women to have some highly prized free time for themselves.

When the mothers were asleep, I crept in to the boys' beds. This stopped abruptly when a mother changed the bedrooms without my knowledge and I found myself in bed caressing a girl. I ran out of the room as fast as I could but she was already awake. Two days later, police knocked on my door. I knew instantly why they were there and, with a great sense of relief, I confessed to all my offences against these children.

I admitted and pleaded guilty to five counts of indecent assault on the boys and accepted the six month sentence without complaint, knowing that this was only the 'tip of the iceberg'. Paradoxically, this relieved me of the dreaded 'poofter' label that I loathed but only because my offences provided the more sinister tag of 'rock spider'.

I was sent to an open prison where there was no form of protection. In common with other child molesters, I was taunted, beaten and injured by men who considered themselves to be superior members of the prison hierarchy. After receiving serious head injuries which necessitated hospitalisation, I was transferred to a prison camp to serve the last four months of my sentence. Within an hour of my arrival, six prisoners kicked me into a state of unconsciousness. The remainder of my stay involved a succession of beatings, verbal abuse and, of course, rapes. I spent most of my sentence in the prison hospital.

I was released suddenly and unceremoniously with no opportunity to talk to a social worker or a psychologist. I had been punished for my crimes by the deprivation of freedom and that was that. I was thrust back into the world with more scars, more bitterness and less trust than before but nothing had happened to improve my social skills with adults, increase self-understanding or change my sexual preference for boys.

I was offered a job in the town in which I previously lived and I accepted it gladly. I offered my services as a volunteer fireman which conveniently provided free accommodation in the fire station. I had been out of jail for less than a week when I heard a knock at my door. There, looking distinctly awkward, was one of the boys who had featured in my list of confessed offences. He expressed sadness that I had told the police about our relationship and complained that my actions had caused him a great deal of distress. I responded that he would have reported me if I hadn't taken the initiative. He assured me that he would not, that he'd missed me during my absence and would like to stay for a while. So, here I was, less than a week out of jail, repeating, with the same victim, the same offences which led to my imprisonment. I didn't have the capacity to resist. He was fourteen years old and the only person in the world who said that he cared about me.

I felt utterly helpless and hopeless. The only way in which I could survive and stay sane was to deny that I had a problem. I rationalised that I never forced boys to do anything . . . they came to me voluntarily. I never hurt them . . . I only touched them. I needed them and they needed me. They liked it . . . why else did they return? Surely that was harmless!

In a small town, you can't keep secrets for long and my history was soon the subject of local gossip. I had to keep my head down and isolate myself as much as possible. The boys in the neighbourhood already knew of my activities and the more curious visited me to find out what I did. Seduction was so easy that I used boys to recruit others. When I saw an attractive boy, I asked my juvenile pimps to find out more about him. I rationalised that, if there was rejection, boys were more likely to report adults than each other. This proved to be an effective form of self-protection and it ensured that I only met curious and willing victims.

My behaviour continued undisturbed until 1987 when I had to return to Australia because my father was terminally ill. Unfortunately, he died a few hours before my arrival and the opportunity to hug him and love him was lost for ever. I mourned the loss of my father but grieved more for the relationship that we never had rather than the relationship that we had. My mother was now alone. She begged me to remain in Australia and I agreed. I found a job as night manager of a hotel in a holiday resort and had been working there for several weeks when I met a seventeen-year-old blackmailer. He identified me as a homosexual, researched my history and demanded payment for silence. I paid but when his demands for money increased in size and frequency, I refused to co-operate. He punished me by waiting until the hotel was busy before announcing, in the loudest possible voice, that I was a 'poofter' who had tried to buy my way into his pants. This made life so intolerable that I had to leave.

I was unemployed for the following six months during which time I stayed with a delightful old lady who had previously shown me enormous kindness. She knew about my problems but didn't reject me. I called her Mum O because she was the kind of person I would have loved as a mother or grandmother. During one of our long conversations, she mentioned that she'd received a letter from Sue, the girl with whom I had shared my bed eleven years earlier. She showed me the letter but I couldn't understand the content. Sue wrote that, after the showdown with my mother, she ran into difficulties with her own family and they dispatched her to Melbourne to live with her grandmother. She said that she was still suffering from the scars of what happened and could never forgive her mother for the part she played.

Mum O sensed my bewilderment. 'What happened? What did her mother do? What does this mean?' I asked. 'You mean you don't know?' Mum O asked with undisguised incredulity. 'Know? Know what? I haven't heard from Sue since the day my mother kicked her out of the house.' 'But you made love to her?' 'Yes . . . but only once,' I said. 'Once was enough, Neil . . . Sue was pregnant. She was expecting your child. Her mother sent her to Melbourne to have an abortion. It was against Sue's wishes . . . she wanted to keep your baby. I thought you knew.'

I was still mourning the loss of my father and now, at the age of thirty, I learned that the only girl who had ever cared for me had conceived my child and I'd lost them both. It was a bitter blow and I was consumed by sadness. Sue had been a very special person in my life. I'd often wondered whether, but for parental interference, we might have married, had children, led a normal life with a regular job and a home in suburbia. How different it might have been.

Over the months that followed, I went into a state of grief for Sue and my dead child. I became conscious of children in the street and whenever I saw ten or eleven-year-olds, I received painful reminders that I, too, could have had a son or daughter of that age.

In January 1988, I went to Sydney to take up the job as manager of an amusement arcade. With the benefit of hindsight, I can see that this was an act of self-destruction because I knew that the amusement arcade was a meeting place for boys. I was constantly surrounded by young, homeless and lonely kids who were prepared to trade their bodies for free games. I could always tell when they had no money because they watched others playing on the machines with looks of envy but they never joined in. Initially, I got into conversation and befriended them. I asked questions about their families and how they were doing at school. I was always attracted to abused boys from dysfunctional families because they responded readily, giving and seeking affection and attention. I offered them a father figure and a shoulder to cry on. They came to me because they needed me. I listened without being judgmental, never turned them away, bought them food when they were hungry, clothes when they were threadbare and gave them money when they were penniless. In many respects, I cared for them better than their parents and that consoled me when I had a troubled con-science. They knew that they could tell me anything and everything. And, of course, in those circumstances it was easy to introduce conversation about sex. I told them about what had happened to me when I was a boy but made it sound exciting. If I began to feel guilty about my intentions, I told myself that I was the only person who cared about them. After all, I was the one who gave them my time, the benefit of my experiences and put some fun into their otherwise miserable lives.

When I finally reached the stage of enquiring whether I could touch a boy's penis, I was seldom rejected. If there was a protest, it was easy to shift the blame. Just as the painter blamed me when he raped me, I told diffident boys that they only had themselves to blame when I introduced sex: they 'knew what I wanted' and they 'came voluntarily'. That silenced them just as effectively as it had silenced me.

I told myself that I wasn't doing any harm: I didn't hurt anyone, I 'only' masturbated the boys and gave them oral sex. After all, they were about twelve to fourteen years old . . . old enough to know what they were doing, or so I thought. I was even proud of the fact that, unlike the men in my life, I never used violence or expected reciprocation. And my delusions of being a good guy continued until I joined the prison programme.

Pepsi was different to the other boys. I was instantly attracted to him. He reminded me of myself when I was young and, some-how, he also represented my own lost child. Pepsi was sad and unloved and he spent whole days and nights at the amusement centre, escaping from trouble at school and abuse at home. His mother was an alcoholic who virtually lived in hotel bars. She failed to keep him clean and adequately fed and clothed. Her first husband had abandoned the family and the three children were violently abused by their stepfather.

Pepsi was so frustrated that he often became angry and lashed out at the world. When he came off worst, he turned to me for comfort. I felt needed and I responded as a father replacement figure. I empathised with him and knew that, for the first time in my life, I really loved a child more than I cared about myself.

One day, I received an abusive telephone call from Pepsi's mother. She was obviously drunk and said that she objected to me providing food for her son; she was his mother and he must eat at home. I explained that I was on duty from 9 a.m. until midnight and couldn't leave the premises to buy meals. Pepsi helped me by collecting take-away food and I shared it with him when the portion was too large. Interestingly, it didn't concern her that Pepsi was with me when he should have been at school.

Her anger diminished and she invited me to her house for a drink. I accepted, gained the confidence of Pepsi's stepfather and brothers and they all invited me to live with them as their lodger. I moved into their home shortly afterwards. It was relatively easy to develop a close relationship with boys who had never received affection or presents from their parents and the only clothes they owned were donated by the Salvation Army. Even small gifts seemed like enormous treats to children who had been so deprived.

During this period, I genuinely believed that I only wanted to be a father figure to Pepsi. This is what he needed and what he enjoyed, but as time went on, I found that I had to battle with myself to keep my hands away from him. I wanted to touch and caress his body and only managed to resist these urges because I loved him dearly and was determined not to wreck our relationship.

My self-control wilted when I took Pepsi and his friend on a camping trip. After the boys went to bed, I sat alone outside the tent and had a few drinks. Alcohol made me depressed and, after a while, I moved inside and lay down at Pepsi's side. I began to stroke his hair, face and body. He stirred but made no protest. Then, I moved my hands towards his genitals . . . and stopped. Suddenly, it was as if I was looking in a mirror but I saw Pepsi as the child in me and I was Tom. My behaviour hit me in the face. I was destroying my one and valuable relationship and, simultaneously, contributing to my own self-destruction.

Pepsi woke up and I burst into tears, apologising profusely, begging him not to hate me for what I had just done. Half-asleep, he was completely bewildered by my emotional outburst. I left the tent and walked away, feeling full of guilt, self-hatred and shame.

When I returned, I found that Pepsi was still awake. I put my arm around him and asked whether he was OK. He assured me that he was and snuggled up close. Neither of us mentioned the incident again.

A few weeks later, Pepsi and I had an argument and he went to bed in tears. I'd been drinking, knew that it was my fault and went to apologise. I lay down beside him, comforted him and let my hands and mouth wander over every part of his body. He neither co-operated nor protested but lay there in frozen silence.

The following day, he was very angry with me and, while I was at work, he disclosed my behaviour to his mother and sought her support. She rejected him, told him to leave her alone and go to the arcade to cry on my shoulder instead of hers. Pepsi said that he never wanted to see that 'poofter' again and, when questioned, he told her what I had done. She clearly didn't believe her son and confronted me when I returned home from work. I felt sick, admitted my guilt and pleaded for her forgiveness. I blamed the alcohol and assured her that it would never happen again. With her own drinking problems and inappropriate behaviour, it was difficult for her to maintain her outrage for long. I also suggested that, if she called the police, her own history of child maltreatment would be revealed and she might lose the care of all three of her children.

When I was certain of my own safety, I confronted Pepsi and asked him why he'd let me down. May God forgive me, I told him that, if the police had been called, I would have been sent to jail then killed by other prisoners and it would have been all his fault.

Afterwards, I deeply regretted putting the responsibility onto his shoulders but it was too late; the damage was done.

I promised that I would never again subject Pepsi to that kind of behaviour and I really meant it; but when I felt depressed and had a few drinks, my good intentions turned to nothing. Sometimes, he rejected my touches but at other times he tolerated them in silence. Every time I molested him he experienced a week of violent moods during which he would be sent home from school for 'uncontrolled behaviour'.

Pepsi was expelled from school after an assault on a boy who called him 'poofter' in front of the class. His life was rapidly becoming a reflection of my own and, with great difficulty, I began to accept that I was the cause of his problems. His behaviour became so disturbed that I persuaded his mother to transfer him to a Catholic boarding school for emotionally disturbed boys. Pepsi returned home for weekends and I fondled him less and less frequently. I had to face the fact that, when I molested him, he always exhibited emotional and violent outbursts when he returned to school and by mid-week, we were receiving complaints from staff. When I left him alone, he was trouble free.

I tried to resist acknowledgment of this connection and with so many other scapegoats to hand, it was easy to blame others for Pepsi's problems. Eventually, I had to admit that his learning, emotional, social and behavioural problems were caused by me . . . not his negligent mother, not his brutal stepfather, but me. I asked myself how I could possibly do this to someone I loved but there was no logical answer.

The boy's behaviour deteriorated rapidly and I found myself accompanying him to the Children's Court on five separate occasions within the short space of a few months. He was charged with theft, then assault, possession of illegal drugs and, finally, with sexually abusing a fellow boarder at school. He stole my Visa card, emptied my bank account and had spent the money on drugs before I realised that the card was missing.

Now, he came to my bed voluntarily, offering sex in exchange for his latest whim. Matters came to a head when he demanded the immediate delivery of a bicycle which I'd ordered for Christmas. I explained that I could not collect it because I'd only paid a deposit on the bike, my bank account was empty and I didn't have enough money to pay the outstanding amount. Pepsi said that if I didn't get it he would tell the police that I'd molested him. He carried out his threat but, after making his statement, he refused to sign the charge sheet and nothing more was said. The next day, I took out a loan and collected the bike.

I worried more and more that I was helping to create a monster. I had to accept full responsibility when, face to face, Pepsi finally accused me of ruining his life. He ordered me to leave his house and never return. There was a calm determination in his voice and I knew that he was serious. I was devastated. I took every pill that I could find in the bathroom cupboard and spent the next three days in the intensive care unit of the general hospital.

Having failed to kill myself, I was offered psychological help and confessed to my problems. The psychologist prescribed Depo Provera, a drug which reduced my sex drive and enabled me to lead a more normal kind of life. My friendship with Pepsi was restored to its former self and he began to succeed at school. I was overjoyed with our joint progress and when I was discharged from the hospital, I took the psychologist's advice to contact Child Abuse Prevention Services for further counselling. The director interviewed me and concluded that I was a caring and worthwhile person who had huge identity problems but, because I wanted to change, would benefit from counselling. She gave me a strong warning however that, because of the laws relating to mandatory reporting, if I revealed that I'd abused a child, the staff would have to report me to the police. I was terrified of returning to jail but also realised that counselling would only be effective if I could be completely honest.

Pepsi pleaded with me not to go ahead with the counselling. I had well and truly convinced him that I would be jailed, killed and that he would be responsible for my death. I did nothing more and managed to control my impulses until the medication ran out. Then, I found myself weakening. I realised that I could not return to the psychologist or Child Abuse Prevention Services and had nowhere to go for help. Sometimes, I stole into Pepsi's bedroom while he was asleep, putting my hand under the sheets to explore his body. He was no longer compliant however. If I disturbed him, he lashed out with verbal abuse and violence. Things came to a head when Pepsi burst into tears and buried his head in my shoulder. I asked what was troubling him. He replied, 'Don't you understand . . . I just want you as my dad . . . only a dad . . . please . . . that's all I want'.

I felt so thoroughly ashamed because, in my heart, that was what I wanted too and I knew that I'd betrayed him. I couldn't risk causing more damage but where could I go for help? How could I seek treatment without being sent to jail? I was trapped in a web of my own making.

I thought long and hard before deciding to go directly to the police. I told Pepsi what I was doing and why. I told him the truth . . . that I was to blame for everything . . . that I'd lied to him and would not be killed in jail . . . that I needed help . . . that he needed to be protected from me and would only be safe if I 'turned myself in'. I emphasised that what had happened was not his fault and I was truly sorry for wrecking his life.

He listened very carefully before replying that I must do what was best. I left the house and walked to the police station. The desk sergeant looked askance when I said, quite calmly, that I wished to be arrested for molesting a boy. Without enquiring about my identity or the details, he said, 'Sir, what you're saying is very serious. I suggest that you go home and think it over. You need to consider the matter very carefully before you make a statement of that sort.' I could scarcely believe what I was hearing. For most of my life, my family had ignored the fact that I had a problem but it had never occurred to me that the police might also prefer to ignore it.

I assured him that I'd thought things through extremely carefully, I was completely sober, understood the consequences of what I was doing and was not prepared to leave until 'some fucking stupid cop decides to charge me with these offences'. Interestingly, when I insulted him, he reacted swiftly and sent for two detectives.

The detectives insisted on interviewing my victim before they would take any action. Although I desperately tried to protect Pepsi from involvement, I failed. I was charged and, farcically, released on bail. I pleaded guilty and received a two-and-a-half-year prison sentence but had to wait another ten crazy months to be sentenced, during which time I remained in the same locality with neither counselling nor psychological support.

The police interviewed all the members of the family and Pepsi was sent to a psychologist for assessment. The psychologist handled the interview badly and asked the boy whether he enjoyed oral sex. Pepsi felt that he was being blamed for what happened, punched the psychologist in the face, ran out of the building and refused to talk to anyone about me thereafter. That worried me enormously because, quite clearly, someone who had experienced such trauma needed professional help to release the anger, express the hurt and expose the inevitable confusion.

I wrote an apology to Pepsi. I wanted him to understand that what happened was not his fault . . . that he was never to blame. I know that Pepsi will blame himself because, even though I was only eight years old when I met Tom, I continue to blame myself for what he did to me. However irrational it may seem, I tell myself repeatedly that I should have stopped Tom, reported him and hated him. To this day, I have neither blamed nor hated him, not even when I learned from my aunt that he was a paedophile who had molested lots of young boys in the neighbourhood.

It has taken considerable counselling to make me realise that the supposedly good times with Tom were not really good and I'd blocked out a great deal of the pain that was the price I paid for feeling needed and loved. With the benefit of maturity, I now understand that my father always loved me but he took it for granted that I would recognise his love in the day-to-day mundane things that he did for me. At eight years of age, I did not understand love and I was easily fooled by a man who was skilled in the art of seduction.

I worry about the trail of destruction that I have left behind. My letter to Pepsi was returned unopened; the family had left the address and I learned that he is in a juvenile detention centre for committing further crimes. I know that at least one other of my victims became a child molester. To my horror, he recently arrived in this jail. I apologised to him for what I'd done. He was surprised by the apology and assured me that he bore me no ill will because although I was the first man to molest him, others followed.

I am afraid to think of how many of the boys I abused might have become adult offenders. How many are in other jails and how many more have not yet been caught? How many men around the world are now reproducing the seduction methods I learned from Tom? It is too awful to contemplate.

I never considered the possibility that what I was doing to boys might affect them adversely in later life because I did not understand what my own victimisation had done to me. Because I could not bear to think about the hurt I suffered as a child, I pretended that it didn't happen (or, if it happened, it didn't matter). God alone knows how many boys I have put on the same lonely path.

I used to tell myself that what I was doing couldn't be bad because it happened to me when I was a boy and 'it did me no harm'. I failed to see the relationship between my childhood experiences and the fact that I was now a lonely and very unhappy man who had already served one jail sentence for paedophilia and was at risk of serving another. I minimised the guilt by telling myself that boys play at sex games with each other and I was actually doing them a service by providing sex education.

Since joining the prison programme, I have realised that what I was doing was very much more sinister. While I convinced myself that I was providing love for boys who needed it, I was merely taking advantage of their distress and loneliness to satisfy my own emotional and sexual needs. The boys needed a friend and father figure; I was looking for sex. I used friendship, food, clothes and money to bribe my victims. It never occurred to me that the boys allowed me to touch them only because they needed the bribes. It never occurred to me that they only said 'Yes' because they wanted to please me and could not risk upsetting me. The boys needed a father, not a lover and I confused the two for my own convenience.

Looking back, I am horrified by what children will tolerate in exchange for approval and attention.

Since being sentenced, I have received the professional counselling that I desperately needed. In the last eighteen months, I have learned more about myself than I learned throughout the preceding thirty four years. Child sexual abuse is like a contagious disease . . . an epidemic which harms everyone that it touches. But unlike most epidemics, very little is known about it and even less is done to prevent and stop it. The sexual abuse of boys is particularly misunderstood. As a child I knew that sex was banned but what was 'sex'? Sex was about men and women and making babies. There was no way that I could have connected 'sex' with what was happening to me in my aunt's bed, in the block of flats, at Tom's house and in my bedroom with other boys.

Responsible adults seriously underestimate male sexual curiosity and the highly sexualised peer group environments in which boys live. Paedophiles condition victims for sex by filling the gaps in knowledge left by parents and the education system. Boys don't report abuse because either they don't perceive what is happening as wrong or they are inhibited by the taboo on homosexuality. When they want to opt out of an abusive relationship, victims are trapped by psychological factors.

Our cultural mores contribute to the vulnerability of boys by depriving them of their fathers' physical affection, approval, hugs, cuddles and good night kisses. Parents often do not realise that their sons need to be loved. Parents also need guidance on how to provide age appropriate sexuality education that will reduce boys' curiosity and open up channels of communication. Until these things happen, boys will continue to be vulnerable to abuse by paedophiles.

3

Unholy orders

All that I know of my early years and family life are the stark facts in a file in the offices of the Department for Community Development. There are no family photographs, no memories, no family heirlooms, no school reports. Although I spent six years at a now notorious boarding school run by a religious organisation, their records merely show the date on which I was made a State ward (some two years after my arrival) and the date of my departure.

I remember nothing of my father. I lack even the vaguest memories of his appearance and personality. My file shows that he worked at a timber mill which was situated across the road from our home, about 35 kms west of Perth. He drank too much, conceived four sons in rapid succession and abandoned all of us when my mother was pregnant for the fourth time.

Although my elder brother was only ten months my senior, he was much bigger and stronger than I. My mother told me that I had three brushes with death in my pre-school years and my brother was involved in all three of them. First, I was locked in an old refrigerator in the back yard and left to asphyxiate. On another occasion, he tried to drown me in a water tank. Finally, he told me to pour kerosene on a fire. I did and, of course, I dribbled it on my clothing and became engulfed in flames. I ran out of the house screaming and headed for the timber mill to find my father. This, of course, increased the combustion and the seriousness of my injuries. My mother claims that my father 'refused' to seek medical treatment for me but I was later admitted to hospital suffering from gangrene and am lucky that my right arm was not amputated.

41

One day, my father announced that he had 'found another job' in central Perth. We left our home and took the train to the city. It seems that my father left my mother, the children and the luggage in the station foyer on the pretext of hiring a taxi. We never saw or heard from him again. The welfare authorities tried to locate him for financial contributions to our upkeep but he took what was left of the family assets, changed his name, left the State and left my mother with a pile of debts.

Not surprisingly, my mother was in poor physical and psychological health and, unable to cope, placed her children in St Joseph's Convent. My only recollection of that period was being dragged by the feet across the floor for wetting my pants.

At the age of six, I was transferred to one of the four boarding schools run by a religious organisation. Although my brothers were sent to the same school, we were separated on the day of arrival. I was allocated a bed in a dormitory for about fifty children. My clothes and shoes were removed and replaced with lightweight khaki shorts and a shirt. This was the extent of our uniform for both summer and winter. The next shock was when I had to line up with two hundred unclad boys to wash under the row of overhead showers. This was supervised by Brothers armed with belts, straps and even wet towels which were rolled tightly into a point and used to whip the flesh of naked boys who moved too slowly, smiled, laughed or behaved as normal children.

I hated and feared Brother X from the moment we met. He was my housemaster, teacher, sports coach, spiritual mentor, mother and father figure. Simultaneously, he was my sexual abuser, tormenter and male adult model for six of my most formative years. He carried a belt which he used for punishing perceived or anticipated misdemeanours. I soon realised that the boys were not and did not have to be cheeky or naughty to suffer humiliating punishment. No-one dared to be mischievous. Normal childish behaviour was not merely discouraged, it was banned. Those who misbehaved were persuaded to expose their crimes at confession but confidentiality was absent and, shortly afterwards, they would be beaten for their behaviour. The matron was a kindly woman but, in a male dominated environment, she had no power or influence. Authority was vested entirely in the Brothers.

Although Brother X was only about 5 foot 6 inches tall, he towered over me. I soon learned that he was in control of every aspect of my life.

I was introduced to violence and sexual abuse on my second

day at boarding school when Brother X took some thirty nude boys down to the river. As a new arrival I was asked whether I could swim. I replied that I couldn't. Brother X, who was fully clothed, then picked me up and threw me off the end of the jetty, calling out, 'Now you can swim'. He laughed loudly as I landed head first in the water. I panicked, choked, struggled and eventually dog-paddled back to safety. I dried myself and went to sit with a group of other boys of my own age. I had only been there for a few minutes when older youths approached me and said that they wanted to show me something interesting. Naked, they took me to a heavily reeded area and, when we were well hidden, began to touch my genitals and each other's. The older boys began to masturbate themselves. I watched curiously, and, to my amazement, they acquired erections. I then tried to copy them. Two of the older boys ejaculated and I watched in wonderment. I was both fascinated and excited but simultaneously terrified that Brother X might find us and beat us for what we were doing. Little did I know that the boys had all been sexualised by the Brothers and I, too, would soon be their victim.

Not surprisingly, I wet the bed and that brought me to Brother X's attention all too swiftly. After lights-out, Brother X patrolled the aisles between the beds, putting his hand under the sheets, ostensibly to ensure that the beds were dry. I soon learned that this was just a ruse to fondle my genitals. Sometimes, the Brother carried me to the toilet and watched closely as I urinated, masturbating himself beneath his robes. At other times, he took me out of my bed, half-awake, half-asleep, and carried me in his arms across the dormitory to his own room. He laid me on his own bed, removed my pyjamas, sucked my penis then masturbated, rubbing the semen over my genitals. This sexual abuse happened several times a week throughout my six years in the school. The Brothers abused the boys and the boys abused each other whenever the opportunity arose. Once you were selected, there was no escape.

I believe that twenty to thirty of the boys in my dormitory were abused at any one time. This was the only 'positive' attention that we ever received and the Brothers maintained absolute control by changing their 'favourites' from week to week. The chosen boys were readily identifiable in class because they were the ones selected to take their work to Brother X's desk instead of raising their hands for the teacher to come to them. When the boy was behind the desk, Brother X put his hand down the boy's shorts and played with the boy's genitals with one hand while masturbating himself with the other. Not surprisingly, the standard of education was poor and my literacy skills are still deficient. It was impossible for early readers to concentrate on 'sounding their phonetics' when they were standing by the Brother's side, his hand down their pants manipulating their genitals.

From the day that I entered school, Brother X was my mother and father replacement. I loathed him and what he did but, unfortunately, I needed approval from this, the only adult in my life. With fifty boys in his care, there was a great deal of competition for the Brother's attention and although I dreaded seeing the black garbed evil predator standing over my bed, I also felt pangs of jealousy when I saw him carry other small boys out of the dormitory into his room. When we were the chosen ones, we were told that we were his favourites and that he would make things easier for us in the days ahead. When I was the current 'special boy', he sometimes moved me to a separate room alongside the dormitory. Brother X then came to my bedroom to have sex or he called me to his own adjacent room. We were not only taken for sex at night-time however, we were used at any time of the day, in the classroom and the toilet block; wherever boys were accessible, they were abused.

Because of our premature sexualisation, even the youngest boys developed pubic hair and found that they had erections and could ejaculate. The erections occurred spontaneously, even when we loathed what was happening. On one such occasion, the older boys forced elastic bands tightly round my penis and when it enlarged, the bands cut into my flesh and I screamed with pain.

Sex was also used as a punishment. I recall that I was belted with a leather strap and sent to bed as a punishment for stealing some lollies from the tuck shop. Longing for my mother, I hid my head under the sheets and sobbed. A few minutes later, Brother X hovered over my bed with his arms outstretched like a bird of prey. He ignored my tears, forced the sheets away from my trembling body and abused me yet again.

In the darkness of the night it was sometimes difficult to identify the predator. As I stirred from my sleep, an adult voice would whisper, 'It's alright, it's only me'. I am aware of being abused by at least three of the Brothers and I suspect, because of the pain, that I put the worst of these incidents at the back of my memory. Even now, I find it difficult to contain my tears when I think of those years. Being the 'favourite boy' did not always exclude me from the regular whippings which all of the boys suffered. 'I have to do it to make sure that the others don't know you're my favourite' was Brother X's explanation. Sometimes the beatings were in private and sometimes in public. I was very small, slightly built and the inadequacy of food ensured that I remained physically under-developed. Our diet consisted predominantly of lumpy porridge, equally lumpy custard, bread and milk.

In common with the boys at other boarding schools we had a very early start to the day. This included church attendance and prayers before breakfast. Throughout the heat of summer and the cold of winter, we wore the same brief shorts and had bare feet. I often wondered what happened to the clothes and belongings that we took to the school because they were never seen again.

The church was not far from the dormitory but we had to run around the back of the grotto along a rough bitumen road covered with sharp blue stone chippings which damaged our bare feet. Forced to run along this road twice daily, blisters presented a common problem and the pain tended to cut down our speed. The Brothers, whose feet were well protected, amused themselves by hitting those who limped and struggled. On one such occasion, a Brother stood beside the rose garden where lengths of newly cut prunings lay on the ground. On the return to the school building, the Brother instructed a boy to move faster. The boy pleaded that he was in pain and lifted his foot to show the bleeding blisters. The Brother responded by thrashing the boy with one of the cuttings, scratching him from head to toe. The mistake he made was in choosing a day boy as his target. Usually, the Brothers were careful not to injure the children who returned to their fee-paying families each weekend. The parents lodged an immediate complaint and the Brother was transferred to Bindoon Boys' Town where, as reports show, sadistic sex and violence were commonplace.

Because I was Brother X's 'favourite' he selected me for the choir. Needless to say, this was merely an opportunity to use me for sex in other situations. I was told to mime because I could neither read music, read the words nor sing in tune.

Being a chorister and an altar boy provided privileges. The choir attended Eisteddfods in Perth which gave children the opportunity to wear good quality clothing, socks and shoes as well as view the world outside our comfortless buildings. We also put on musical performances of Oklahoma and Gilbert and Sullivan operas such as 'Pirates of Penzance', 'Mikado' and 'Trial By Jury'. These public performances gave the community the impression that the Men of God were doing wonderful work in raising discarded orphans to

45

appreciate cultural life. These were the only 'good times' in my memory of that time and even they were marred by the fact that Brother X gave me the female theatrical roles and dressed me as a girl.

In common with our counterparts at the other boarding schools run by the same religious group, we were used as slave labour for the building of the church and the maintenance of the buildings. The Brothers never soiled their hands or extended their muscles; they merely acted as slave drivers to ensure that the children undertook work that should have been given to men. Although I was only six when I arrived at the school, I was allocated to the building programme and carried the bricks, the paving stones and the bags of cement. There was no mechanisation and no regard for children's safety. Accidents were commonplace. Psychological abuse was used to ensure that every ounce of effort was squeezed out of the boys. Small, young children like myself were belittled and jeered and urged to compete with bigger and older boys. Given that Brothers had already built a whole Boys' Town of magnificent edifices at Bindoon using child labour and had received public adulation for their efforts, they had no conscience about using six-year-olds as labourers or eleven and twelve-year-old builders. And when children were injured, little attention was paid to their medical needs. When I grew taller, I was given the task of painting and cleaning religious statues, many of which were twice my height.

One day, with no prior warning, I was told that new 'foster parents' would take me home for Christmas. I was extremely nervous because, having spent so much of my time in an institution, I did not know how to behave in a family setting. My anxiety turned to panic when I walked outside to the family's car and found twin girls of my own age sitting on the back seat. I could not recall seeing girls before and to the best of my knowledge, I had never talked to one. The family took me on my first ever trip to a drive-in cinema and through sheer excitement and nervous exhaustion, I slept throughout most of the film.

My foster parents placed me in the same bedroom as the girls and, for the first time, I saw comfortable beds, pretty curtains, bedspreads and carpets. I also saw, to my absolute horror, that the girls had lost their penises and testicles. When I undressed for bed the girls were equally concerned to note that I had peculiar appendages which they lacked. We were in the process of investigating these interesting physiological differences when their mother walked into the room. She stepped back, raised her hands in horror, called me a bad, dirty-minded little boy and said that I would have to return to school immediately. I knew that I would be subjected to sadistic punishment if I returned prematurely and I cried and pleaded and complained that it 'wasn't fair, it wasn't all my fault' and I wanted to stay with them for ever and ever.

My pleas were to no avail and when my 'foster father' returned home from work, he agreed that I had betrayed their trust, violated their daughters and, being a danger to others, must be returned to the Brothers there and then. As I knew that I was returning to a disastrous Christmas, I decided that I wanted to punish my supposed 'foster mother' for what I had lost. As I left the house, I took her watch from the table and put it in my haversack.

The Brothers were standing at the door as we drove up to the school. I had been silent throughout the journey and I shivered with fright as the foster parents left me in the car and spoke to the Brothers in private. When the 'foster parents' left I was taken by the arm and pushed into the office. The Brothers yelled, screamed and swore at me, using obnoxious language to indicate that I had let them down, that I was an ungrateful wretch, that they had been burdened with me because my own uncaring mother had abandoned me and not surprisingly so, because I was an evil, worthless sinner. This tirade was, of course, accompanied by uncontrolled belting with a wide leather strap as well as their fists.

Two days later, the theft of the watch was discovered. On this occasion, I was strapped and punched until I was senseless. Then, the Brothers sent for the police. I sat, alone, trembling in the empty room and my heart almost stopped when I saw the police car arrive. I expected to be taken to jail but the policeman said that, on this occasion, I would be 'let off with a caution' but must 'never do it again'.

For the rest of the holiday I was the only boy remaining at school and the Brothers either ignored me or abused me. I was desperately lonely and afraid. I slept alone in the dormitory, had nothing to do, no-one to talk to and no-one to play with and I was only eight years old.

A very nice couple, Mr and Mrs Newton, took me to their home for the next school holiday. I befriended Les, a neighbour who taught me to do things I had never done before. We played 'war games' and pretended to be soldiers. I wore Mr Newton's old Army hat from World War II. It had a bullet hole in the crown. I rode a 'Billy cart' and pretended that it was a tank. Having had no previous opportunity to play in the street and practise safety skills, I was a danger to myself, pedestrians and other vehicles. On one occasion, I picked up speed as I rode down the hill and crashed straight into Mr Newton's car. He was very upset and I was terrified that, once again, I would be returned to school as a punishment for my misbehaviour.

When I tried to ride Les' bicycle, it was even more exciting and more catastrophic. I forgot the whereabouts of the brakes, crossed a busy road junction in peak hour traffic and crashed into a wall, wrecking the bike. Mrs Newton witnessed the accident and yelled at me in panic, but on this occasion, I realised that I had found someone who really cared about my welfare. Despite the associated traumas, the Newtons continued to invite me to their home. Only recently I realised that, in their loving household, I never wet my bed, while at school I suffered from chronic enuresis. This has worried me. I know that I received the affection and attention that I needed from Mrs Newton. Did I also wet the bed to gain the attention of Brother X? For a long time it never occurred to me that my bedtime problems related to my fear of the Brothers. I told myself that I liked their sexual attention because it was the only attention I received. This led me to blame myself for their sexual misbehaviour, however irrational that may seem to the reader.

I was very proud when the Newtons collected me in their new car, my friend Les waving, smiling and beckoning me to the rear seat. Happiness terminated quite suddenly with the unexpected death of Mr Newton. No-one explained what had happened and I just cried and cried.

Shortly afterwards I made friends with a boy named Joey who worked with the pigs and the chickens. We were in separate dormitories and had different teachers but we sought each other's company outside the classroom. Together, we decided to run away.

One night, I stirred in my sleep and looked up to see the black shadowy outline of Brother X silhouetted against the dimmed light of the dormitory. I pretended to be asleep and escaped under the blanket, holding my breath in the hope that he would move on and select another child. He didn't. He pulled back the bedding, lifted me out of my bed and carried me across his arms to his bedroom.

The next day, Joey and I tried to kill a chicken by pulling its neck. We were not sufficiently strong and the bird refused to die. Then, we heard a Brother coming towards the chicken house and, in fear of our lives, we threw the chicken into the pigsty where it was eaten by the ravenous animals. The terrified bird made so much noise that we knew it would attract the Brother's attention. We ran as fast as we could and did not pause for breath until we reached Queens Park. By that time it was already dark and we decided to find somewhere to sleep. The only accessible place was in a hollow tree. We were cold and afraid of the dark and tried to light a fire from a pile of twigs. It was a relief when dawn broke and we could leave our hideaway. We set off walking again although we had no particular venue in mind.

Inadequately clad, shoeless, cold and hungry, we responded gratefully when a lady invited us into her home for a drink and something to eat. She realised that we were runaways and, unknown to us, telephoned the school to inform the Brothers of our whereabouts. The Supervisor came to the house to collect us and return us to the school. He made us stand outside his office for a long time before ordering Joey to go inside. He closed the door and I covered my ears as he thrashed my friend on his bare buttocks. Joey screamed. I then heard the Supervisor Brother thump the boy across the head repeatedly with his fists. I stood there nervously, realising that I was about to receive the same treatment.

The Supervisor opened the door and ordered me into the room. Only then were we asked why we had run away from the school. I looked at Joey, his face red, swollen and tear-stained and we both said, spontaneously, that we didn't know the answer to his question. The Brother sent Joey limping out of the room and again closed the door before repeating the question. I reiterated that I had no explanation for my abscondment. He then turned and, with the full force of his body, hit me so hard that my feet left the ground and I flew through the air, landing head first on the corner of his table. I lost consciousness as the blood poured from the top of my head. The supervising Brother disregarded my injury, shook me until I recovered and thrust me outside his office, threatening that he 'hadn't finished with me yet' and would send for me again after I had taken advantage of the opportunity to pray for my sins. There was no medical treatment for our injuries and, to this day, I have a sizeable scar and dent on the crown of my head from the blow inflicted by the Brother in charge of the institution.

Later, Joey and I were taken to the handball court. The Brother said that he would give us one last chance to explain our behaviour and, when we could not, he told us to strip naked and fight each other. He threatened that if we did not beat each other 'to pulp' he would do it for us. We knew that he meant it.

By now, I was beginning to recognise the hypocrisy of the 'Men of God' who constantly reminded us of our daily sinfulness and threatened us with hellfire and damnation. We were constantly assured that God was 'Love' but there was no love to be found in God's institution for children. I began to sense the conflict between what the Brothers said and what they did. They claimed to make enormous sacrifices for us but there was no evidence of this and they clearly experienced no joy in their parenting role. Hypocrisy was most apparent in their dining room and kitchen. While the boys ate frugally and hunger was a feature of everyday life, the Brothers ate lavish meals of roast meat, roast potatoes, vegetables and puddings washed down with liberal quantities of wine. The smells from the kitchen tantalised our nostrils and stimulated saliva. In the meantime, boarders were constantly dehumanised, reminded of their dependence, their illegitimate sinful birth or their abandonment by uncaring families. We were often told that, if we complained about our lot, we would find ourselves in the street, unwanted and homeless. The hypocrisy was most evident when visitors arrived. We were quickly provided with new, respectable uniforms including shoes and socks. These disappeared just as quickly when the visitors left. The Brothers were highly competent at giving the public a good impression of their institutions and their dedication to the care of disadvantaged boys.

At the age of eleven, I spent a holiday with a family in a mining town east of Perth. This was very exciting because it involved travelling by train with a policeman who was very kind and took me to the dining car to buy chocolate. I had never travelled so fast before and I particularly enjoyed the sensation of going in and out of tunnels.

I was very apprehensive about meeting my new foster family but when we arrived the policeman gave me a hug, lifted me on his shoulders and said, gently, 'Come on, little chap, we'll find you a new family. You'll be happy here.'

My new foster parents greeted me with a big hug and introduced me to their son. We took a taxi to their home and, en route, they explained that they had invited me to live with them to provide a playmate for their boy. Their son's hostile glances made it clear that he neither wanted nor needed my friendship.

The family lived in a neat, cosy little house almost within walking distance of the railway line. I enjoyed the simple pleasures of life such as waving to the passengers on passing trains.

My foster father was often away from home for several days at a time. My foster mother, a very large, bosomy woman, continued to check my bed for signs of wetting, just as the Brothers had done.

On one occasion, when her husband was away, she woke me up, carried me to the toilet and, instead of returning me to my own bed, she put me into hers. She removed my pyjamas and began to stroke my body. She removed her nightdress, laid me face down on top of her and sucked my penis. Although I enjoyed the sensation, I was scared that her son might find us and tell his father and I would be returned, once again, to school.

Whenever my foster father was away from home, my foster mother took me into her bed. She called me her baby, nursed me and told me to suck her breasts. In return she sucked my penis.

In the meantime, I was enrolled at another school run by the Brothers. There I met my dear old friend Les who told me that he lived within cycling distance and would be pleased to see me at his home. The joy of seeing Les again offset the very bad news that I had failed the aptitude test and would have to be in a class with children much younger than myself.

My foster brother refused to lend me his bike and it was some time before I could persuade another boy to ride the five miles to Les's house with me sitting on the crossbar. It was a wonderful reunion and we reminisced for hours about our adventures and the kindness of my earlier 'foster mother' Mrs Newton.

During the Christmas holiday, I underwent surgery at the local hospital and returned to school after the term had already started. As I walked into the classroom, I recognised my new teacher. It was Brother X, my previous tormenter. When he saw me he called my name and instructed me to take my work to his desk. Once there, he moved me to his side behind the desk where he put his hands down my shorts and abused me, just as he had done before.

A short time later, a policeman called at the house and took me to the police station. He placed me in an unlocked cell and told me that I was to be returned to Perth. I wondered why but no explanation was given. Had my foster father discovered what was happening in his bed when he was taking the trains to Perth and Adelaide? Had his son 'told'? I dared not ask.

The next day, another uniformed policeman accompanied me on the train but the journey was full of sadness and we scarcely spoke. A fight broke out in the dining car and the attendant sought the policeman's help. He handcuffed me to the bed in the sleeping compartment and left me on the floor.

Happily, I never returned to my former boarding school. I was one of the few lucky ones who escaped from that religious system and went, instead, to a 'receiving home'. During that time I met my mother for the first time in seven years. I recognised her instantly and I was full of happiness, certain that she had come to take me home. Instead, she told me that she had a new husband who did not want the children from the first marriage. Furthermore, the two little girls standing behind her were introduced as my half-sisters. Despite the disappointment, it was wonderful to see my mother again and we sat on a bench and talked and talked until it was time for her to go.

One month later, I learned that my foster mother wanted me back. The whole family met me at the railway station but my foster brother was as sulky and unwelcoming as ever. I made another friend, Michael, and through him began to date my first girlfriend, Laura. We fell in love but our happiness was short-lived. My foster mother discovered our relationship and banned me from seeing the girl again.

Throughout this time I continued to be obsessed with sex and I masturbated whenever the opportunity arose. What worried me, however, was that I found myself fantasising about sex with Brother X as well as with my foster mother. Eventually, she caught me masturbating and she was very angry indeed. I responded in anger, declaring my undying love for Laura and, in a fit of blind fury, my foster mother phoned the authorities and declared that I was 'unmanageable' and must be taken away.

On this occasion I was flown back to Perth and the Captain allowed me to sit beside him. This was the most exciting day of my life and I did not want the journey to come to an end. Far from being ashamed of my 'unmanageable' status, I was convinced that I was the luckiest boy alive. Two weeks later, I was dispatched to a very large household full of foster children. Before and after school, we were given responsibility for mowing the lawns, weeding the garden and keeping the house in order. There, I began to take an interest in philately, using my spending money to add to my collection. One day, the owner of the local stamp shop took me round the back of the counter on the pretext of showing me his stamp album. Out of sight of other customers, he placed his hands down my pants. Thereafter, he exchanged sexual touching for free stamps for my collection.

At this foster home I had my first birthday party and received my first presents, a watch and a small radio. These gifts were highly prized and I still have them. I also went to a State High School and, for the first time, wore long pants and a school uniform. I felt very important and the girls surveyed me and giggled as I walked into the classroom.

I had no idea how to behave in this mixed community but, with no sexual distractions, my literacy skills improved and I began to write letters to my mother. She never replied but I always hoped and dreamt that one day the family would be reunited.

Sometimes I was advised by the social worker that my mother intended to visit me. I dressed in my best clothes, scrubbed my face, combed my hair, sat by the door and waited . . . and waited. At the end of the day, I retreated to my room, swallowed hard to hold back the tears and pretended that I didn't care. But I was heartbroken. This happened again and again and, eventually, I had to accept that my mother was untrustworthy and I learned to ignore the announcements.

One day, I saw her in the congregation at the Cathedral. My heart leapt and I rushed towards her expectantly. She turned, recognised me and said, 'Get lost'. I burst into tears, ran out of the Cathedral and wept all the way home. My foster parents saw my distress and called the social worker. She visited my mother and discovered that I now had five half-brothers and sisters living at home while my own brothers continued to live in religious institutions. My mother's new partner, Jim, had banned her from contacting her sons from her first marriage. My mother was living in a very violent relationship which she tolerated because, without his income, she would not be able to support their young children.

Soon afterwards, I recognised one of my long lost brothers on the beach. He gave me my mother's address and I decided to visit her. I found that Jim had left her and I could now stay the night when I wanted to see her.

Two more girls arrived at the foster home and I fell in love with Pat. On Sundays, she dressed up in her best clothes to go to church and my eyes were upon her throughout the service. My affection was not reciprocated but I now had a social life and met other teenagers. I knew nothing about girls, nothing about sex (other than from my experiences with my abusers), nothing about reproduction and menstruation and I made some disastrous blunders which caused me enormous embarrassment.

One day, I was staying at my mother's when Jim returned. He was a big bully of a man. I found him in the kitchen, my mother huddled in a corner with her arms above her head protecting herself from his blows. He was surprised to see me and, although much smaller in stature, I took advantage of that surprise and waded into him. I pushed him towards the door, told him to 'Piss off and leave my Mum alone', and threw his bags outside with him. To my amazement he left quietly and never returned.

My first job was chosen for me by the State welfare department and I started work as a French polisher at the age of fifteen. This job lasted only a few days because my social worker walked into the factory just as the men were initiating me into my apprentice-ship. The ceremony involved painting lacquer on my genitals. The social worker concluded that this was not a suitable environment for an innocent young boy and she removed me instantaneously. My second job was as a furniture removalist.

I ran away from the foster home after breaking a window in a fight with another boy. The foster father was angry and hit me. I retaliated and pushed him through the door.

The remainder of my adolescence involved a succession of jobs, fights and girls. There were no meaningful relationships until, at nineteen, I met Teresa. We liked each other, respected each other and her parents welcomed me. Being a good Catholic girl she wanted to save sex for marriage. It was while I was staying at their house that I committed my first offence against her younger sister. Emma used to hop into my bed each morning. I snuggled up to her and enjoyed the hugs and the cuddles and the warmth of our relationship. Emma was nine years old, trusting and spontaneous. These morning treats had happened regularly for more than a year when, one day, I was sexually aroused and placed Emma's hand on my penis. She returned to my bed the following day and I viewed this as her willingness to participate. Thereafter, sexual contact became addictive and I used every available opportunity to touch her. Looking back, I realise that Emma had much in common with my childhood. She was lonely, needed approval, warmth and com-fort. I provided all of these, but at a price.

I married Teresa when I was twenty one. At the wedding, I met my older brother for the first time in seventeen years. This made me very happy because my family was now reunited and I had a beautiful wife and a home of my own. Nine months later, my adored Teresa was pregnant and although parenthood had not featured in our plans, we were both confident that our love was strong enough to overcome whatever hardships were ahead. My parents-in-law were less than enthusiastic and gave strong warnings about financial problems but I did not listen. Teresa stopped working and I came home to my wife and a beautiful daughter whom we both worshipped.

Our second child was conceived a year later. I was working as a welder and volunteered for overtime to make ends meet. I had no trade qualifications and attended night school to improve my position.

I was present at the birth of our son which was a tremendously moving occasion. Soon afterwards, Teresa felt the need to return to work. She took a job at a hotel which involved evenings and weekends. When she was working, her younger sister came to stay for the weekend to help me to care for the children. Given my earlier sexual abuse of Emma this was obviously a dangerous arrangement.

On one of her visits, I took Emma into my bedroom, undressed her, kissed her and had sexual intercourse with her. She was terribly distressed and I urged her to keep my behaviour secret from my wife and her parents. I was confused and scared by what had happened. I didn't know what to do.

Two months later, my father-in-law telephoned and instructed my wife and I to go to his house immediately. When I arrived, he sent Emma to play outside with the children. Then, he asked me whether it was true that I had raped his twelve-year-old daughter. At first, I denied it but eventually admitted my guilt and he called the police. I was charged with unlawful carnal knowledge and, surprisingly, my father-in-law bailed me out and took me back to his house.

I told my lawyer that I had a problem and wished to plead guilty because I needed help. She told me not to be so stupid, 'If the Judge hears that, he'll think you're a menace to society and give you a hefty jail sentence'. I received a fine of $200 and no help whatsoever. We spent the whole of that week at Teresa's grandparents' house but we slept separately and I knew that our marriage was in ruins. My wife no longer trusted me and viewed her sister as my mistress. She constantly asked why I loved her sister more than I loved her. I tried to tell her that I adored her and our children but my words seemed shallow in the light of the evidence. She expected a logical explanation for my behaviour but there was none.

My wife decided to 'stick by me for the sake of the children' but there was no joy in her decision. My court case and legal expenses left us in financial ruin and we had to sell our beloved house. My father-in-law allowed us to live rent free in a family property that he was renovating but this was to help Teresa and his grandchildren and I found myself ostracised by her entire family.

The following Christmas, there was an attempt at reconciliation. I wanted desperately to apologise to Emma, Teresa and her parents but they refused to listen. I was silenced with, 'We don't want to hear about it ever again. We want to forget.'

Teresa and I were having serious problems with our relationship when we learned that she was pregnant again. I was delighted but she was not. I thought that she would change her mind when our second beautiful daughter was born but she remained tense and unhappy. Teresa often tortured herself by asking questions about my relationship with her sister—did she please me better? What was it that made her so attractive? She could not understand my conduct and neither could I. Our sex life diminished to the extent that I resorted to masturbation in the toilet. Teresa now had no affection for me and could not bear to kiss me on the lips. My work was also stressful. I was employed on laying a pipeline and my lack of concentration resulted in a number of 'near miss' accidents. It was dangerous work and there were several fatalities on the site, including the loss of a youth in a landslide.

It was about this time that I began to 'fondle' my eldest daughter. This started when my wife was at work and I gave the children a bath. I never touched either of my younger children improperly nor have I had the desire to do so. I don't know why this is unless it relates to the fact that I was present at their births and the bonding was stronger.

I confessed my crimes to a chaplain in the Army Reserve and told him that, having molested my young sister-in-law, I had now turned my sexual attentions to my own daughter. He asked me whether he could talk to my wife. I said 'Yes' and he telephoned Teresa in my presence. She asked to speak to me. I knew that she would be angry but her cause for concern was not what I expected. Her rage was not because I had violated our child but because I had been disloyal to her family by disclosing our private affairs to a 'stranger'. She made me promise that I would never speak of it again.

We continued to live together but led separate lives. We did not argue or fight but were distant and polite. I invested more of my time and my emotional self in my children. I took the girls to their dancing classes, helped with their concerts, coached my son's football team and won 'Coach of the Year Award'. This was the first award I had ever won in my life and I was proud of it.

In 1984, I persuaded Teresa to take a holiday with me without the children. When we were alone together it seemed that a heavy load was lifted and we could talk, laugh and even hold hands spontaneously. But when we returned home, the pressure returned again. At about this time my wife, an adopted child, located the whereabouts of her own father and attempted to contact him by phone. He rejected her instantly. This was extremely traumatic because it smashed her dreams of reunification with her own flesh and blood. She could not discuss her feelings and withdrew further into her own world. All of the time, I blamed myself for what was happening but I felt powerless to restore our relationship to its former self.

Much later, I began to suspect that my wife was having an affair. Quite suddenly she began to 'work late' and, on two occasions failed to come home at all. She made excuses that she had 'stayed with friends' but her stories were blatantly untrue. I phoned her at work when she should have been there and learned that she was supposedly sick or had taken the day off. I could not challenge her and, full of sadness, I turned increasingly to my children for emotional support.

One day, I received a call from her employer to tell me that Teresa was on her way home because she was very ill. When she failed to arrive, I was worried and went out to look for her. She arrived home at midnight and I asked, 'Where have you been? I've been really worried.' When she replied, 'I've been at work', I knew that she was lying and I 'hit the roof'. I told her about the message from her employer. She lied again and said, 'I fell asleep in the car'.

I hoped that, given time, our relationship could be restored but my wife saw more and more of her lover and less and less of her family. We planned holidays with the children but, on each occasion, she found a reason to stay at home. As time went on, I increasingly focused my attention and affection on my eldest daughter. For nine whole months, I knew that she was at risk, that my feelings for her were becoming sexual and I needed help . . . but there was nowhere to go. How could I go to our general practitioner and tell him what was happening in my head? How could I tell a priest? I knew of no counselling facilities for sex offenders and was convinced that no-one would understand.

Eventually, I took the dreaded step and again fondled my daughter. She did not reject me and it became addictive. Sometimes, I went to her room at night and took her into my bed. Now, it was much worse than before and I used her as a mini adult and a source of comfort.

Teresa and I planned a holiday in Malaysia with the children but once again she changed her mind at the last moment. As the children and I flew off to Kuala Lumpur, my wife took a flight to New Zealand, supposedly for a holiday with girlfriends but, in reality, to meet her lover. Before they left I met her boyfriend and asked if he intended to look after the children because I was clearly not coping. The boyfriend said that he was too young for the responsibilities of marriage and children and merely wanted 'a bit of fun' with my wife. When I repeated this to Teresa, she did not want to believe it, became angry and attacked me.

The flight to Malaysia reminded me of my childhood flight to Perth and I asked the flight attendant if the children could meet the Captain and view the flight deck. To my great joy, and theirs, he agreed. The remainder of the holiday was wonderfully happy except for one thing: we all shared a family room at the hotel and I treated my daughter as my wife throughout our entire stay. I found opportunities to keep her for myself when the younger children went to the swimming pool and I told her to keep my behaviour secret because, if she didn't, I would certainly go to jail. In focusing on my own need, I was oblivious of the harm that I was doing to my child.

When we returned home, my wife announced that she was leaving me. I should have been prepared for that but I was not. I had always hoped that things would improve between us and now I lapsed into a state of grief. The announcement came on our wedding anniversary that Teresa was going to live with another man and she intended to leave the children with me.

On the twentieth of September, a group of colleagues stood talking while waiting for a crane to set down a pipe. A car drove up and a woman walked towards us. She screamed, 'You dirty rotten bastard. You've been interfering with your own daughter.' I turned and came face to face with my wife. My workmates stood aghast. Teresa blushed red with embarrassment and turned, walked back to the car and drove away. I ran to my vehicle and followed her home. I told her that I needed help. She asserted that she 'didn't want outsiders to be involved' and we had to sort this out for ourselves. I ignored her, phoned 'Parent Help' and waited for three hours for help to arrive.

A social worker collected my daughter from school. She ran into the house, hugged me and said that she was sorry. I told her that she had done the right thing and that she should tell the whole truth. She did, but I regret to admit that I didn't. I was terribly confused and had battles going on inside myself. I was both terrified of going to jail and terribly ashamed of what I had done. I wanted my problems to come out in the open but I lacked the courage to reveal them.

Later, I drove down to the Child Abuse Unit and told them everything. I was 'scared shitless' and didn't know what to expect. I was charged with two counts of incest and spent Christmas in prison. I was not allowed to speak to my daughter. She sent me the message that she loved me and wanted to see me but, in the meantime, I received a six-and-a-half year jail sentence. I remember my first day at Fremantle Jail very clearly. As the gates shut behind me, I had the same feeling of entrapment that I experienced so many years ago when I entered the Brothers' school. Certainly those years with the Brothers provided me with the skills to survive in an adult penal institution.

I was released from jail in 1988. I was not allowed to contact my children for the first three months of freedom. Then, I returned to my old job and started coaching the football team again. My children gradually began to trust me but there was no possibility of restoring my relationship with Teresa. I was alone and lonely although I had one friend, a single mother who had sons aged eleven and three.

I got along especially well with Andrew, the eleven year old, and he enjoyed coming to the sports club with me. During the long summer break, his mother had to go into hospital and they both persuaded me to take Andrew into my home for the duration of the holiday. I resisted but they persisted and, in the end, I gave in.

I liked Andrew a lot and valued his company. He was a great comfort to me at that time. I was feeling sad and he was a good listener.

It was during the second week that I took advantage of Andrew. He was asleep on the sofa and stirred as if he were dreaming. As I watched him I felt a strong urge to stroke his body and gently unfastened his pants. He woke up suddenly. I shall never forget the look of shock and horror on his face. He cried, said that he was scared and wanted to go home. I delayed taking him until he recovered his composure. I was appalled by my behaviour and suddenly realised that I had done exactly what the Brothers had done to me in my bed at boarding school.

Three months later, the boy's uncle contacted me and enquired whether I had sexually molested Andrew. I knew that he did not want to believe the allegation; why else would he have informed me? I denied it, of course, but two weeks later I received a visit from two child protection officers. I again denied the offence but I was charged, bailed out by my brother and, almost a year later, sent to jail for a further three years.

My own children disowned me. I denied the offences and called my victim a liar and that I deeply regret. I would dearly like to apologise to all three of my victims but I am not allowed to make any kind of contact.

In jail, I joined an offender treatment programme. This was beneficial in helping me to see my life in context and understand the triggers which had caused me to offend. I have long realised that there was a strong element of self-destruction in my behaviour. I destroyed all of the relationships that mattered to me. I have to keep telling myself that I am an offender and will always be at risk. It is vital that I give myself frequent reminders of what I did, what it has done to me and the children and wife I dearly love.

I now have a support network in place and know that, although temptation is still likely to occur, there are people to whom I could turn for help when the going gets tough.

While I was still in jail, I contacted the Brothers hoping to find information about my childhood. Brother Y assured me that his colleagues had 'done their best' to care for me but there were no reports or records and I was merely a name in a register. A short time later (July 1993), Brother Faulkner published a public apology to former boys for what had happened at the hands of members of his congregation.

Any satisfaction that might have been gained from the apology was marred by the Brothers' excuses that allegations were 'exaggerated' and were, to some extent, 'understandable' given the 'hardships and standards pertaining at that time'.

No, Brother Faulkner, the 1960s were not 'hard times' and I ask myself why men of the church should be excused for breaking their vows and committing the most heinous crimes which, over the years, must have damaged thousands of lives, created hundreds of paedophiles and generations of incestuous families. Significantly, while many of their victims have been incarcerated in the country's jails for repeating the offences they suffered at the hands of the Brothers, the main perpetrators were protected by the church and have never been apprehended. Some are still teaching.

I became especially angry when I searched through Department of Community Development files. There, I read and photocopied a social worker's report dated 13 February 1968 which said, 'Following a distress call, I visited the child's foster mother who told me that

Robert has been exposing himself. At first she ignored him, but, when it persisted, she scolded him. He was afraid and apologetic. Robert is a difficult boy, sullen, uncommunicative and bad tempered. He argues with any friends that he has and never smiles. Robert told his foster mother that while he was at [school] he and the other boys, including his older brother, David, were made to strip by the Brothers, and engage in sex play with each other. Robert wet his bed until six months ago. It appears that he has had no sex education. The family seems unable to cope with this.'

The questions I would like to ask are these: 'Why, oh why, dear social worker, did you choose to ignore this cry for help? Why did you leave me there when you knew what was happening? Wasn't it your job to protect children? Why did you by your very silence, allow these men to continue their evil practices, violating and corrupting generations of innocent boys? Were their young lives expendable because children are less important than the reputation of the Catholic Church? What are your reasons?'

4

Children in the 'care and protection' of the State

> How can you ask a child to be honest and true
> When he can only judge by what he sees in you
> (lyric; author unknown)

When I was invited to write a chapter for this book, I knew that I had to respond. I am not a writer and have never done anything like this before in my life. I thought about it for a very long time before making a start and the more I thought, the harder it became to put pen to paper. I had no difficulty in putting the early part of my life together. I recall my childhood experiences with alarming clarity. It was only as I moved on that it became harder and harder. What I mean is that I'd pushed aside the very painful memories of my life in children's homes and I found myself becoming very angry when I had to revive them. I'd buried these memories for so long that I didn't want to dig them up and confront them. And yet I was driven by the urge to continue because I have a duty to expose what happened to me and the hundreds or even thousands of children who, like me, were abused while in the care of State child welfare authorities. I seek no payment for my contribution to this book nor do I want compensation. Money cannot bring back my lost childhood. Nothing could compensate for the hugs, the reassurances, the approval, the genuine warmth of affection that children need and I never had. Nothing could ever compensate for the unnatural things that I, and others like me, had to endure while under the control of the so-called 'child care' authorities. No fistful of dollars could undo the damage to my life and put it back together again. All that I need is for the New South Wales Government to acknowledge that, yes, this really happened to children in their care and, yes, they were responsible for our safety and well being. And I need to know that, although this happened a long time ago, someone is sorry that it happened and those responsible for child welfare are taking much greater precautions to ensure that it does not happen again.

In this chapter, you will notice that I do not use the surnames of the house-parents who maltreated me. They are all now dead but their children and grandchildren may be alive and I would not wish them to be recognised by their unsuspecting family members. I have no wish to cause any more hurt to innocent people.

My story begins when I was three years old. I recall a house which I regarded as 'home'. I slept there but seemed to spend most of my time wandering around the streets of Paddington in central Sydney.

I have very hazy memories of a woman who, with hindsight, must have been my mother. I slept in her bed but my recollections are of a cold, affectionless person who never cuddled or hugged me or showed even momentary concern for my well being. I do not recall sitting on her knee, hearing stories or nursery rhymes at bedtime or having the kind of bath-time play enjoyed by children in caring homes.

I used to get into trouble when my mother had men in the house. I can still hear the words and her angry tone of voice when she told me to 'Fuck off' and get outside. I never understood what was happening or why I was being rejected but I knew that I had to get away quickly to avoid trouble. And get out of the house I did! So far as my mother was concerned, it didn't matter where I went so long as I left.

One day, I returned home to find that the front door was locked. I went to the back door and that was locked too. I knocked at the neighbour's house. She was a kindly old soul who would sometimes take care of me when my mother was out with her men friends. I began to get really upset when she wasn't there. I'm not sure what happened next . . . I probably went to look for my mother but I ended up at Circular Quay and spent a lot of time around the ferry terminal. I have no idea where I slept or how long I lived in the open. I do recall searching dustbins for waste food.

I have very clear recollections of the man who took an interest in me. He seemed to be very kind and bought me a pie and some chips. I can still remember how good they tasted after eating from dustbins. I paid a price for the treats however because he then took me into the public toilets to 'play' with him. My memory tells me that this happened three times and on the third occasion, the man was arrested by police and I was taken to the police station.

I have very pleasant recollections of caring policemen who bought me lots of lollies and ice-cream and let me play on their typewriter. These were tremendous treats to a kid who had been starved of affection and attention. I had to stay at the police station for quite a long time. I don't know whether they failed to locate my mother or whether she abandoned me completely but I enjoyed being there and didn't want to leave. I never saw or heard of her again.

Eventually, I was taken to a very big house which was to be my new 'home'. This was the beginning of my sixteen years of life in the 'care' of the child welfare authorities. I had no birth certificate and no possessions. I was three years old.

Royalston Boys' Home

Royalston Boys' Home at Glebe was a very large and frightening institution. I was a small, undernourished, insecure and frightened child who, having lost the only adult in my life, now faced hordes of taunting, laughing and staring children who were highly amused by my arrival, hand in hand with a uniformed policeman. I held onto him very tightly and didn't want to let go. I felt safe with police and tried to prevent him from leaving me. As he tried to pull himself free, I clung more tightly. Then, an elderly woman saw his predicament and separated us, roughly grabbing me by the shoulder and forcing us apart. She told the policeman to leave quickly. I felt that I was losing a protector and I screamed and demanded to go with him. The woman told me to shut up and, of course, I cried all the louder. She said that if I didn't stop crying, she would give me 'something to cry about'. She then whacked me on the buttocks, pushed me out into the yard and closed the door behind me. I found myself facing what seemed like hundreds of noisy and aggressive children, most of whom were very much bigger and older than me. This was my introduction to institutional life.

I was terribly distressed and it took me a very long time to 'settle down' and accept that this was my home and I had no other. No-one ever talked to me about what had happened and why I was there. No-one mentioned my mother. In common with other residents, I assumed that I'd been naughty and this notion of innate wickedness and worthlessness was promoted by the staff. It was a long time before I realised that there was no escape and no-one was coming to collect me and take me home to Paddington.

The sexual abuse began on the very first day that I was 'in care' and continued until the day that I left. At the bottom of the yard was a two-roomed school which was attended by boys of five years upwards. We pre-school children were made to sit on the verandah and keep ourselves occupied. We had no toys and no adult supervision other than that given by the teacher who, from time to time, left the two classrooms to reprimand us for misbehaving. He was a very big man who always carried a cane in his hand. This was not the walking stick kind of cane used by people with disabilities, it was the kind of striking cane seen in pictures of schools of the Dickensian era.

The teacher carried his cane everywhere that he went and he used it liberally for striking those who committed the most trivial misdemeanours. I quickly learned that this man had to be taken seriously and, after several whacks on my bum, I became a very quiet, suppressed little boy.

I also learned that the teacher had a very strange habit. He would call out the name of one of the boys sitting outside on the verandah. When he called out my name, I expected to be punished for doing something wrong. Instead, the teacher smiled down at me and said, 'Johnny, get the keys out of my pocket'.

I have very clear recollections of finding that, when I put my hand in his pocket, the pocket lining was missing. The teacher saw my surprise and told me that the keys were 'farther down'. I put my small arm deeper into his pants and discovered that he wore no underpants and my hand was on his penis. The teacher sensed my panic and smiled down at me reassuringly.

'That's my boy' he said, 'now, tickle me.' Of course, I obeyed his instructions. It never occurred to me that I could do otherwise. After a while, he said, 'That's enough'. He then rewarded me with a biscuit.

There were nine young boys on the verandah and I soon discovered that all were asked to search for non-existent keys in non-existent trouser pockets. This happened several times a day on five days of the week. We never talked about it . . . we just did it. It was in our interests to keep this violent man in a good mood and we particularly liked the special cakes and biscuits that we received after we had carried out his wishes.

After school, all the boys played out in the yard until it was time to shower. Every pre-school child was allocated to an older boy who was given the job of undressing and washing him. The reader may think that this was a good idea . . . providing an opportunity for older children to take responsibility for young, dependent children who needed a one-to-one caring relationship.

That was not the rationale behind the arrangement however. The reality was that the older boys were given absolute responsibility for the care of their charges because there was no adult supervision in the shower area. There was only one master on duty and he stayed in the yard keeping an eye on the older children. As a consequence, the big boys could do whatever they wanted with the young ones and they had no fear of being caught because no-one else entered the showers until the young children had left. Furthermore, they knew that the young boys would not report them because they had no-one to tell! In fact, at the age of three and four, we thought that, as what was happening was so commonplace, it must be 'normal'.

I always had the same boy to 'look after' me. His name was Wayne. To me, he seemed like an adult although he was probably only twelve or thirteen years old. What I can say with absolute certainty is that he washed me in exactly the same way on seven days of the week throughout the whole of my stay at Royalston Boys' Home. First, he undressed me, then himself and we went into the shower together. He then soaped all of my body, spending an unwarranted amount of time handling my genitals. When my penis became stiff, he used this as the signal to push his finger inside my anus. This always hurt and I hated it. He then rubbed his own body all over mine. When he finished rinsing me, he knelt down, gave and then demanded oral sex.

Wayne also liked to urinate over me and, sometimes, he asked me to reciprocate. This happened day in and day out and I knew of no other method of showering. 'What about the other boys?' you may ask. 'Couldn't they see what was going on?'

Yes, of course they could. In fact, what made me absolutely convinced that what we were experiencing was 'normal' was the fact that the showers were open and the other boys were doing the same kinds of things with their young charges. We accepted it and even liked some aspects of it given that this was the only individual attention and the only pleasant touching that we ever received.

After showers, we were dressed in our pyjamas and had tea before going to bed. At some time during the night, the older boys woke us up for sex. I do not need to give you the details . . . you will be able to guess what happened.

I think that I spent about a year in Royalston, at the end of which I was well and truly sexualised. And I was still only four years old.

Waverley Cottage: my second State home (aged four to seven years)

Although there was no preparation for my departure from Royalston, I was already thoroughly institutionalised and had no strong feelings about moving to Waverley Cottage. Waverley had the facade of being a large but 'normal' home in that there was a house-father and house-mother, Mr and Mrs K, who were responsible for children in three dormitories. One dorm catered for the under fives and the remainder housed mixed age groups.

I already knew several of the boys at Waverley because they had also lived at Royalston. One of them, Patrick, became my friend. He was the same age as me and slept in the next bed. We also shared the ignominy of being habitual bed wetters which made us very unpopular with our house-parents.

We were showered and dressed by the house-mother until her husband decided that she was too lenient and he would have to 'take control' of us. Patrick and I knew that we were heading for trouble because we had seen other boys being belted for minor misdemeanours (and I do mean belted . . . using a heavy leather strap with a large brass buckle which penetrated the skin). When he was in a really bad mood, the house-father also closed his fists to strike the boys and when they were lying helpless and stunned on the ground he kicked them around the room like footballs.

Under the new arrangement, our house-father woke us each morning. As I peered through bleary eyes, my first view of the new day was the sneer on his face as he put his hands under the blankets and asked, 'Well, have my two little pisspots done it in their beds again?'. I quickly came to my senses and felt the dreaded warm, wet patch under my back and thighs. When I responded, 'Yes, sir', this was the signal for him to drag me out of bed by the scruff of my neck, my feet several inches from the ground. He then paraded me up and down the dormitories telling the other boys to 'look at this . . . he's too bloody lazy to go the bathroom. Isn't he a disgrace?' And all the boys would meekly answer, 'Yes, sir'.

Patrick suffered the same treatment. We were deeply upset by the public humiliation and the insinuation that we deliberately wet the bed. We both tried desperately hard to stay dry and often vowed that we would keep each other awake to stop it from happening. This never worked of course . . . we fell asleep and, the next morning, the result was always the same.

After the public ridicule, the house-master took us to the bathroom. There, he ran the cold tap, stripped off our pyjamas and dunked us in the cold water. This was tolerable in summer but, in winter, Mittagong was a very cold place indeed.

When we were blue with cold, shivering and our teeth chattering, we were dragged outside and left to stand wet and naked in the middle of the back lawn. In winter, our feet sank into the early morning frost. We were ordered to stand still until our tormenter ate his breakfast and gave us permission to move. I have no idea how long we stood there but, to a four-year-old, it seemed like an eternity. Our feet were covered with chilblains and the pain was often unbearable. One day, quite by accident, Patrick and I discovered that we could keep our toes frost free if we urinated on them. This gave us something to laugh about and, somehow, it provided an opportunity for secret defiance.

One morning, we were taken to the bathroom and stripped in the usual way. We gritted our teeth in preparation for the cold water but found, to our surprise, that the bath was warm. We couldn't believe our luck. I can't recall exactly what happened that day but I do remember that the two of us were standing in the bath when our house-father took hold of both our penises, one in each hand and said, 'Haven't my two little boys got nice looking doodles'. He fingered them both and then performed oral sex.

We must have been in the bathroom for a very long time because, when he dried and dressed us and himself, the others had already eaten their breakfasts and left the dining room. We ate with the house-father and, during the meal, he constantly reminded us that we must never tell anyone about what had happened. It was our special secret. The promise was unnecessary because we seldom left the cottage and had no-one to tell.

The house-father also told us that, if we were good boys and stopped wetting the bed, he would give us the treat of having a warm bath every morning. And, of course, it was a great treat compared with the dunking and the exposure to frost and cold wintry winds on the back lawn. So, Pat and I tried even harder to stay dry but we failed and the punishments continued, interspersed with occasional warm baths and sexual molestation as the reward for being good. The difference now was that our house-father locked the bathroom door, undressed and climbed in the bath with us. This was the signal for oral sex and fondling. It was the only gentle touching we received from him and we liked it so much that we did it to each other when no-one was around.

Pat and I were referred to as the house-master's 'pets'. I soon realised that he had several 'pets' and we all had to play with each other's genitals while he observed and instructed us. Paradoxically, this is the only time that we felt safe; it was the only activity which did not result in derision and violence. And, of course, the older boys did it to the little ones and, even if they were caught, they were never reprimanded. The house-father merely winked, laughed and said, 'I'll see you later'.

Most weekends, the house-mother returned to stay with her relatives in Sydney. It was on a Saturday night that I woke up to find the house-father shaking me. 'Wake up Johnny,' he said. 'Are you wet?' I was relieved to confirm that the bed was dry. He lifted me out and carried me into his own room where he sat me on the bed. As I looked around, I was surprised to see three older boys, all naked. I felt uneasy and looked up at the house-father for reassurance. There was none.

'Take your pyjamas off, Johnny. We're going to have fun,' he said. I was apprehensive but obeyed. The house-father then slipped his own clothes off, put them on the back of a chair and stood directly in front of me. 'Come on . . . kiss it,' he ordered. No-one had ever kissed me and I didn't know what he meant. The boys saw me hesitate and called out, 'With your mouth, idiot'.

I leaned forward and quickly brushed my face against his genitals. The house-master was furious. I had never seen him so angry. He clearly felt that I was being deliberately disobedient, humiliating him in the presence of his admiring audience of apprentices. 'Not like that, you little bastard! Do it properly.'

He grabbed my head and forced open my jaw, ramming his penis to the back of my throat. I panicked because I couldn't breathe. Then, my guardian turned to the other boys and said triumphantly, 'See, I told you I'd get it all in'. I choked and glanced sideways at the other boys looking for sympathy. Instead, I saw that their eyes were dancing with excitement, and the greater my distress, the more they were amused. One of the boys was Wayne . . . yes, the same Wayne who had molested me in the showers at Royalston.

'Why don't you put your balls in his mouth too sir?' he asked.

My house-parent laughed, 'I've already thought about that but . . . his mouth is too small'.

He lay me on the bed, face down, raised my buttocks with my legs spread-eagled, told the boys to hold me down and, with them cheering him on, he raped me. He assured me that it wasn't going to hurt but I trembled so much that I could not keep still. None of the punishments previously inflicted on me had prepared me for the pain which followed. I can't describe it. I'd never felt anything remotely like it before. It was as if a red hot knife was splitting my body completely in two. I screamed, 'Please sir, don't sir, it hurts'.

I struggled and cried and the more I struggled, the more he hit me until, finally, I could struggle no more. 'Shut up and stop whining you little bastard. Someone will hear you,' he said. Suddenly, one of the boys said, 'Sir, he's bleeding'. My attacker did not pause to investigate but replied, 'Don't worry about it. He'll survive.' The agony seemed to last forever. I couldn't understand what I'd done wrong to deserve this terrible punishment. After all, I hadn't even wet the bed.

When Mr K had finished with me, he told the boys, 'Oh boy! That was great . . . '. This was an expression that I was doomed to hear all too often.

He then ordered Wayne to get the camera. 'Now,' he said, 'it's your turn. I want the three of you to do it with him and I'll take shots of you. Now, who wants to be first?' And because they all liked to please him, they all volunteered. And as each boy raped me, my house-father photographed them.

By this time, I desperately needed to use the toilet.

'OK, you'd better go . . . but hurry because we haven't finished with you yet.' In the toilet, I realised that I was bleeding profusely. I ran back to the house-father in a state of panic. 'Oh, stop whingeing boy,' he said. 'You won't bleed to death.' He then placed a large waterproof sheet on the bed and lay me down on it. As I write this, I can still feel the cold clamminess of the rubber on my back.

I looked up at the faces surrounding me, desperately seeking some kind of reassurance but there was none. I was terrified. 'Right,' my house-parent said, 'seeing that you love wetting your bed, the four if us will piss all over you. And from now on, we'll do this every time you and that other little prick Patrick wet your beds. Is that understood?'

'Yes, sir.' He was, of course, a man of his word and the following night, Patrick was raped and degraded in exactly the same way. We were then five years old.

This combination of rape and degradation continued throughout my remaining three years at Waverley Cottage. On weekdays, I was abused in the bathroom and at weekends, when the house-mother was away, I was abused in the bedroom. As time went on, Mr K demanded more and more deviant behaviour. Sometimes, we had to cover his genitals with golden syrup or honey, sprinkle him with choc-bits and lick them. Then, this was repeated with the older boys. And all the time, we were photographed.

Looking back, I realise that I was more afraid of the older boys than of the house-father. In many ways, their demands were more deviant, more brutal and more persistent. I formed the impression that they wanted to outdo their master and he, in turn, gained satisfaction from hearing of their exploits. They didn't just urinate on the little boys, they made us drink it. I found that I could cope with this only if I shut my eyes, held my breath and swallowed quickly so that I could neither taste nor smell the noxious fluid. One day, Wayne got angry when he caught me doing this. He regarded it as 'cheating'. As a punishment he saved and made me drink three small Coke bottles full of his urine.

Shortly afterwards, Wayne was transferred to Berry Boys' Home but, alas, Sam remained and he was bigger, older and even nastier than Wayne. Sam used to grab us by the testicles and squeeze them if we refused to comply with his demands. He hung on until we passed out with pain. On one occasion, I plucked up the courage to complain to the house-father. He sent for Sam and asked whether my allegation was true. Sam grinned and admitted that it was. 'Show me exactly what you did,' instructed Mr K. And Sam grinned even more as he squeezed and pinched until the tears ran down my cheeks. 'Is that all that he did?' asked the house-father sarcastically. 'Yes, sir.' Mr K shook his head in disgust and ordered me out of the room. 'And stop complaining,' he said. 'Don't you know that Sam is only playing with you?'

One of the house-father's favourite tricks, which Sam re-enacted, was to prevent uncircumcised boys from urinating by winding elastic bands tightly around their foreskins. Eventually, our penises swelled up and turned purple. Removing the elastic was a very painful process.

One night, Sam was supposed to be reading a story to us but he was sitting by Colin's bed playing with the little boy's genitals under the sheet. No-one took any notice because it was such a regular occurrence. I don't know what Colin did to annoy Sam but the older boy suddenly leapt into the air and hit Colin in the mouth, yelling, 'I'll teach you a lesson'. He took a rubber band from his dressing gown pocket and put it on the left hand index finger of the little boy. Colin complained that it was too tight but no-one took any notice . . . in fact we forgot all about Colin until the following morning when he woke up screaming, clutching his hand. His finger was now unrecognisable . . . just the bare bone covered by a thin film of badly discoloured skin.

The house-father heard Colin's cry and came to investigate. Colin was rushed to the hospital where his finger was amputated. Sam lost none of his privileges and was not even reprimanded.

Later, I was out in the back yard talking to my friend Patrick when one of the boys ordered me to go to the house-father's room. There, I was accused of picking flowers in the front garden. I pointed out that I had only been at the back of the house and Patrick could confirm that I hadn't been near the flower bed. 'Are you accusing Sam of lying?' the house-father asked. 'Sir, he must be,' I said, ''Cos I didn't do it . . . sir . . . honest.'

I knew as soon as I'd said it that I'd made a mistake. The house-master grabbed me and the jug cord and used it as a whip on my bare buttocks. I tried to wriggle free but the more I struggled, the more violent he became. He hit me until I collapsed then kicked me for good measure.

That night, I was covered in cuts and bruises and felt utterly helpless. It took me a long time to fall asleep and when I awoke, I found myself standing by the house-master's bed with a butcher's knife in my right hand. Realising that I wanted to kill him, I dropped the knife and ran like hell back to my bed.

By the time I left Waverley Cottage, I was thoroughly trained in every conceivable (and inconceivable) form of sadistic sexual practice. Not a day went by without being subjected to some form of psychological as well as physical and sexual abuse at the hands of the man employed by the New South Wales government to care for me and protect me.

The older boys who emulated him were, of course, as much his victims as the younger ones. At the age of eleven or twelve, they were already dehumanised and they showed no conscience in circumstances in which a conscience could be expected. Like circus animals, they had been trained to please their master, irrespective of what he desired. They were his 'right hand men'. They were ascribed limitless power over the younger children but they also had to take responsibility for many of the caring tasks. They took us to church on Sundays. Routines in children's homes revolved around religion and prayers. The older boys also walked us over the six mile route to and from the medical centre (No. 2 Hospital Home) when we were sick and they often had to shower and dress us. And, of course, they fondled us whenever there was an opportunity . . . and there were opportunities daily . . . before and after sports, phys. ed. and swimming lessons, in the toilets, changing rooms and dormitories and behind bushes in the garden. Everyone was obsessed with sex. Sometimes, as a special treat, we were allowed to go with the older boys to the children's films at the cinema. And when the lights went down, that was the signal for more sexual touching. While John Wayne shot the big bad guys, the older boys from Waverley Cottage abused the little guys. We never complained because most of the time we enjoyed it. After all, it was the only pleasant touching that we knew.

Turner Cottage: my third State 'home'

At the age of seven, I was moved to Turner Cottage. The move took all of three minutes because I had no possessions and the cottage was on the same site. Although there was no fence between the two houses, there was an invisible barrier which could not be crossed. The school-aged children at Waverley attended Mittagong Primary School whereas Turner Cottage children attended classes in their own schoolroom. I have never been able to work out the logic of this.

I soon began to realise that my house-parent at Waverley had been a 'cream puff' compared with the new one. Mr L's very appearance made me tremble. He had a nice, kind, compassionate wife but she was frightened of him too. She made it clear that she dare not comfort the little boys in case she was discovered and accused of being 'lenient'. Everyone said that she was very sick and spent a lot of time in hospital. Whatever the reason, she was seldom at the cottage with her charges.

I lived at Turner for six years, four of them under the control of the same house-father. During that time, I estimate that I received at least 1460 beatings, usually with a cane designed specifically for the task. In addition, when he was very angry, Mr L grabbed and whipped us with the cord and plug from the electric iron.

I soon realised that the house-father derived great pleasure from our distress and while I could not control his violence, I could reduce the level of satisfaction that he gained from being sadistic. I gradually taught myself to move my mind out of my body so that I felt no pain and produced no tears.

What horrified me most was that the house-master meted out the same punishments to his own two sons. I could understand why this man hated the rest of us . . . I had been told often enough and believed that we were worthless rejects of society. But why would he brutalise and degrade his own family? I felt terribly sorry for these boys. Jason was thirteen and a quadriplegic. A diving accident left him confined to a wheelchair. Robert was the same age as me. They were both likeable lads and I was glad to have Robert as my friend.

Their father absolutely terrified me and, as a consequence, I wet the bed unremittingly and was punished and humiliated even more than before. Every morning, he yanked me out of bed and held me in the air by the collar of my jacket while my pants were pulled down to the ground. He then pointed his cane at my penis saying, 'Look at this, boys. You wouldn't think that something as tiny as this could make such a lot of water, would you.'

And, of course the boys, ever eager to please, laughed and replied, 'No, sir'. He would make me bend over so that he could poke his cane into every crevice, calling out, 'Ooo . . . look here . . . he's even wet here . . . and here'. And the boys peered obediently.

Mittagong then had three 'orphan homes' and an additional eight homes for what were often referred to as 'wayward boys'. On one night of the week, six of the house-fathers met at Turner Cottage. On that night, I was taken from my bed and displayed before these men as the cottage 'pisspot'. They investigated every part of my body to see where I was wet. The performance concluded with a caning on my bare buttocks. That stung but the greatest hurt was caused by the public humiliation.

'I bet you don't have any seven year olds who still wet their beds', the house-father would say. And they all agreed that even the most wayward boy did not share my appalling habit. In the meantime, my house-parent would be tapping and poking at my genitals, running the point of his cane along my body.

I had been at Turner Cottage for about three weeks when, one night, I woke up and found the house-father stroking the front of my pyjama pants. I remember this occasion because he bent over and kissed my forehead and no-one had ever done that before. He then sat on my bed and stroked me saying, 'You've got a nice little stiffy there Johnny'.

"Yes, sir.'

'You do like me doing this to you, don't you Johnny?'

'Yes sir.'

'I'll tell you what, if you're a really good boy, I'll come and play with you more often. Would you like that?'

'Oh, yes sir.'

'That's my boy!' he said and put my hand inside his pants which were already open.

'Ah, that's lovely,' he said. 'You are a good boy!'

And, of course, I was happy because I wanted to be good and I wanted to please him and be kissed and cuddled. I would have done anything to receive his approval. And when he asked whether I liked him stroking me, I said that I did. And I was telling the truth. For four years, I had been taught by every man that I knew that you never get into trouble when you're playing in their pants. And I was certain that if I had rejected what he was doing, he would become angry and punish me.

Suddenly he asked, 'Do you know what suck means, Johnny?' I said that I did.

'Where did you learn to suck, Johnny?'

'Waverley Cottage sir.'

He smiled. 'Do you like sucking?'

'Yes, sir.'

And then, I was asked to demonstrate what I could do. As he got up to leave, he said, 'You must never tell anyone about this or you'll get into big trouble. Do you understand?'

'Yes, sir.'

Possession of the secret gave me a new feeling of confidence and I enquired whether, from now on, he might view my bedwetting a little more leniently . . . at least until I was a little older. He laughed. 'I really don't care about you pissing in your bed,' he said. 'It gives me the chance to rub you all over in it. I love it when you're wet.' To this day, I've never been able to understand how anyone could derive pleasure from handling a body soaked in urine.

When the house-father left, I naively believed that life was going to be easier from now on. I sensed that the man who kissed me was a different person to the one who slashed my buttocks with the cane. I slipped down the sheets and slept easily for the first time in years. Unfortunately, my optimism was short-lived. The following morning, I was paraded around the dormitories and humiliated just as before. One day, the house-father's son, Robert, had nothing to do. We sat on the schoolroom steps and talked. Suddenly, out of the blue, Robert asked, 'Do you like my dad, Johnny?'. I thought very carefully before I responded but I sensed that he wanted the truth. 'No, I don't. He hurts me.'

Robert smiled and said, 'I know . . . I hear him ranting and raving every morning. Can't you hide your wet 'jamas?'

'No! If I did, he'd soon find them and belt me even more for trying to avoid being punished.'

'I suppose you're right.'

He looked at me directly and said, 'He belts me too you know'. He lifted his shirt and showed me the welts on his back. I was astonished and enquired whether it hurt very much. 'Not now,' he said. 'It's three days old.'

'Why did he do that?'

'He doesn't need a reason. I didn't leap out of bed fast enough when he told me to get up. He's like that. You don't have to do anything wrong. He hits my brother too.'

'You're kidding!'

But he wasn't.

'How could he hit someone who is helpless in a wheelchair?' I asked.

'He does lots of terrible things to him,' Robert said and for a few moments we sat in silence.

I was shocked. I had learned to accept brutality as part of my lot in life as an unwanted child but it had never occurred to me that people would do this to their own children.

'Does he visit you at night?' Robert asked tentatively.

'What do you mean?' I asked, suddenly remembering my promise of secrecy.

'He does it to me,' Robert said. 'And he tells me that he does it to all the little boys in the cottage. I wondered whether you were one of them.'

I admitted that I was 'one of them' and that his father visited me about three times a week. Robert was aghast. 'But he does it to me three times a week as well,' he said. 'And he does it to Jason too.' Again, although I had learned to accept sexual molestation as 'normal' I was shocked that the house-parent did this to his quadriplegic son.

So, Robert and I compared notes and this sharing of information helped us to feel very much stronger. We had a great deal in common and formed a close bond. Together, we laughed at our tormenter and, somehow, that diminished the power that he wielded over us.

Inevitably, we got around to showing each other what Robert's father did to us. Robert said that he loved me and I said that I loved him but we were fondling each other when we said it.

I had been at the cottage for about six months when, one night, I was allowed to stay up late with Robert and four older boys. We had no idea what we had done to deserve this privilege but we felt quite important when the others were sent to the dormitories and we remained in the lounge. At about nine o'clock, the house-father collected us, took us to his bedroom and closed the door. On the bedside table was a bottle of chocolate sauce and jars of 'hundreds and thousands' and similar small sweets. 'Great, we're going to have a party,' I said to Robert, not really knowing what a party was.

His father confirmed that we were indeed having a party and he was going to teach us some new games. He instructed us to remove our clothes and then he laid a large canvas on the bed.

'OK kids . . . now close your eyes and when someone touches you between your legs, hop on the bed.'

We all closed our eyes and waited apprehensively. Mr L touched his own son and Robert climbed on the bed and lay down on his back. Then, his father picked up the bottle of chocolate sauce and poured it over the lower half of his son's body. He then sprinkled the sauce with 'hundreds and thousands' and ordered us to lick him clean.

Tony, a new boy, was horrified.

'What? Lick his bottom?' He winced and stepped back.

The house-father grabbed him by the neck and pushed him on the bed snarling, 'Of course from around his bottom. Did you think I would want you to lick his ears?'

The startled child was thrust onto Robert's body and told, 'Now, lick'. Then it was my turn. I was relieved when it was over and enquired whether I might be allowed to go to bed. It was late and I was tired.

'No you can't. I've got better games for you,' he said.

The house-father orchestrated appalling acts . . . boy to boy. At the end, we all had to kiss Ron, the oldest participant, and we learned that he was going to be Mr L's bed partner for the night. We felt sorry for him because all but the new boy knew what that would mean.

The house-father had absolute control over twenty boys. He was

God and the Devil rolled into one and we were terrified of displeasing him. If he'd told us to jump off Sydney Harbour Bridge, we would have done it.

Not all the boys were involved in sadistic sex however. Some escaped consistently but it took me a long time to realise why: they were the boys who had visitors. I never had a visitor throughout the whole of the time that I was in the care of the State and, as a consequence, there was no-one to whom I could complain about my living conditions.

What distressed me most is that Mr L involved us in doing the most degrading things to his disabled son. We were even forced to watch him rape the boy. As I write, I am still angry about this but, at the age of seven, I had already accepted rape as something that we had to tolerate. I suppose that when something awful happens on a daily basis, you have to find ways of coping with it and you either ignore it or you join in. I couldn't afford to show that I was upset by it because that would expose me to further ridicule and abuse.

What is even more disconcerting is that I really loved this man. I wanted so much to please him. I wanted him to be a 'real father' to me. I wanted him to love me.

I mentioned earlier that, once a week, five other house-fathers met with Mr L at Turner Cottage and it was during these meetings that I was removed from my bed and paraded, prodded, poked and humiliated in their presence. It never occurred to me that they were sexually excited by this performance until, one night, I arrived to find them all naked. I was instructed to fondle them and perform oral sex on every one of them in turn. Throughout this, my housefather laughed and joked and took photographs of what was happening. He later showed me the prints to provide positive reinforcement for my involvement. 'Look here, Johnny, you were doing a great job on him!' he would say. And this was the only kind of praise I ever received at Turner Cottage.

The other men in the group showed me photographs of them having sex with their 'favourite boys' from their own cottages and they bragged about the pleasure the boys provided. What this told me was that the behaviour I experienced at Waverley and Turner Cottages was being reproduced in at least five other neighbouring boys' homes.

Thereafter, whenever I went to the weekly meetings the men were already undressed. One night, after completing the rituals expected of me, one of the men grabbed me and admired my bottom.

'Have you ever fucked this one?' he asked the house-father.

I looked directly at him, praying that he would say, 'No'. But of course, he didn't. 'Regularly,' he replied.

The man who was holding me said, 'Good . . . because I want him'.

'Take him! He's all yours,' replied the house-father.

I closed my eyes and my whole body trembled in fear. As I felt the man approach I spontaneously tightened my muscles. This was regarded as an act of defiance and I was whacked on the buttocks for my lack of co-operation until my resistance collapsed. The pain was unbearable. I can feel it now as I write. The tears welled up in my eyes but I dare not cry. I couldn't let them see that they were hurting me. But I thought that I was being torn apart.

When this man had finished with me, he told the others that I was 'great'. He then picked me up and passed me on to the next man . . . and the next . . . and the next until all six men had raped me.

'Is he bleeding?' asked one with a hint of concern in his voice.

The house-father examined me cursorily and declared, 'He'll live'.

These six men raped me every week thereafter. Eventually, they became bored with it and wanted different kinds of 'fun'. The house-father introduced them to his son, Robert and he too was shared around. Their desire for more revolting practices increased.

They inserted foreign objects into us. They started out with table tennis balls and, week by week, graduated to larger and larger items such as carrots, cucumbers and even hard boiled eggs. The more difficult the task, the more excited they became.

One day, when I was taken into the room, I saw that these nude men were examining a yard broom. They looked very funny and I assumed that they wanted me to sweep the room with it. I was wrong. Their challenge for the evening was to see who could push the broom the greatest distance inside my body without killing me. I was in absolute agony. I decided there and then that I was going to run away. But where could I run? To whom?

I was now nine years old and knew that these men had a boss and he lived in the Superintendent's House on another part of the estate. And when everyone had gone to bed, I crept downstairs and escaped through the lounge window onto the back verandah. It was only when I faced the cold night air that I realised that I was dressed in my pyjamas and had nothing on my feet. I was tempted to go back to my room to dress but I realised that, if I were caught, I would be in serious trouble. I decided to stay safe and run. I ran past Waverley Cottage and saw the light in the house-master's bedroom. I hoped that he wouldn't see me so I ran faster until I was safely through the main gates. Then, I had a 'stitch' in my side and had to slow down.

It was very scary along that dark road. I wasn't used to being alone and I suddenly became conscious of the rustling of the trees and the shadows made by the moon as it passed eerily behind the clouds. What was it that the older boys had told me about dangerous strangers? Didn't they grab kids from behind bushes and do bad things to them? I imagined that there were evil strangers in the hedgerow and I ran even faster. After five miles, I collapsed in a panting heap on the doorstep of the Superintendent's House, my heart beating so loudly that I feared it might burst. I knocked on the door. It seemed to take an age before there was any sign of life. I feared that he was away for the weekend and my effort was for nothing. But no, he came to the door and he looked a kindly man. I was instantly relieved and felt sure that he would help me.

'Hello, young man! Who are you?' he asked.

I began to explain why I was there and he invited me into the kitchen. He sat me down on the chair and pulled another up to the table so that he was sitting close to me.

'Now, tell me what this is all about. Start at the very beginning. Why are you here, Johnny?'

I hesitated. He put his hand on my shoulder and said, 'Come on, son. Something serious must have happened for you to run all this way in your pyjamas.'

So, I opened up my heart and told him everything.

He wasn't shocked. He didn't say that I was lying or that he didn't believe me. He let me finish without interruption and then asked, 'How many men did you say there were?'

'Six, sir.'

'Do you know their names?'

'No, but they're house-masters at the other cottages, sir.'

'How do you know that?'

I told him about the photographs and the way in which these men bragged about their sexual achievements with their 'favourite boys'. The Superintendent listened to all of it. He then put his elbows on the table and his hands under his chin and looked at me in silence for several seconds.

'Johnny, I think you've got it all wrong,' he said very calmly and gently.

I looked up at him and said, 'I'm telling the truth sir . . . honest. Cross my heart and hope to die . . . those men took the yard broom and they put it . . .'

This was when he smiled. I remember it so clearly because this wasn't the kindly smile that I expected. It was a tight, mean smile in which his lips curled at the edges. He said, 'I'm sure that the house-masters never intended to hurt you Johnny. It must have been an accident.'

He looked directly into my eyes and before I had the opportunity to protest further, he said, 'You know that you're Mr L's favourite boy. Hasn't he told you? He only does these things to you because he loves you. And when he punishes you he does it for your own good. Hasn't he told you that?'

I cast my mind back and had to admit that I'd often been referred to as the 'favourite boy', the house-father's 'pet'. And yes, he had often told me that he was punishing me to make me into a better person; he beat me and humiliated me to stop me from wetting the bed. And certainly, all of the men told me that they liked me . . . after they raped me.

I was very confused. Could it have been an accident? Had I imagined it? Maybe the men didn't intend to hurt me. Maybe it's OK for grown-ups to shove brooms up kids. I had no other life experiences with which to make comparison. After all, the house-father involved his own son . . . so maybe it really was normal for adults to behave in this way.

By the time the Superintendent had finished talking to me, I was convinced that it was all a terrible misunderstanding on my part . . . that I was the one with a problem because I had failed to appreciate what my loving house-father was doing for me.

'Show me where these men hurt you,' instructed the Superintendent. So, I dropped my pants and showed him. And when the Superintendent said, 'Bend over', I bent over. He opened up the tender anal passage with his fingers and said, 'It's a little red . . . but you're not bleeding. Does it hurt?'

I lied, 'No sir, it's better now.'

'Good boy!'

He turned me round to face him and touched my penis.

'Does that hurt?'

'No, sir.'

'Good, now what about here?'

He touched my testicles.

'No sir, it doesn't hurt.'

He then picked me up and sat me on his knee and began to stroke me gently.

'You know Johnny, you're a very pretty boy. No wonder your house-father loves you.'

At this stage, I should have suspected his intentions but I didn't. After all, this man was the big boss responsible for all of the children's homes. He wasn't like the house-masters. He didn't growl. He had a gentle voice and a gentle touch and he won my confidence. I liked him. And when he told me to get undressed, of course I did as I was told. He then put his arms around my buttocks, pulled me close to him and whispered in my ear, 'I wish you were my favourite boy Johnny. I could really love you.'

He hugged me for a good five minutes and I thought that it was wonderful. I had never felt so secure in the whole of my life. I felt that no-one could hurt me while I was being protected by this man . . . not the house-masters . . . not the older boys. In his arms, I was safe from the whole world.

A little later, he lifted me back on his lap and questioned me about the fine detail of what the house-masters did to me. Quite cleverly, he persuaded me to categorise which behaviours I liked and didn't like. During this detailed interrogation, I revealed that I hated foreign objects most of all and human 'rape' was marginally less painful than a broom handle or a cucumber. By this process of elimination, I eventually revealed that I liked being fondled. He stroked me gently and said, 'Like that?'

He did not wait for an answer.

He admired my genitals and said, 'My, you are getting into a big boy, aren't you Johnny'.

He took me back to Turner Cottage the following night, having arranged that, from now on, I would spend every weekend at his house. This sounded preferable to weekends at Turner Cottage with the house-masters' groups and I was very happy that I'd been chosen for these visits.

When we returned to the cottage, I was sent immediately to my bedroom. The two men talked elsewhere and although I struggled to eavesdrop on their conversation, their voices were blurred. The following day, I was again belted for wetting the bed but the house-father never referred to my late night visit to the Superintendent. He merely confirmed that, from now on, I was to be collected after school on Friday afternoons and I would spend every weekend with 'the boss'.

The rest of the week was the longest in my life. I pestered the house-father continually about what I should take and what I would play with when I got there. He replied that I wouldn't need any clothes. I wondered whether there were some already at the house. How would he know my size? It seemed a little strange but I rationalised that he probably had access to the clothing store.

After school on Friday, I positioned myself so that I could see the Superintendent's blue car as it came along the driveway. I don't know what I expected but I literally jumped for joy when he arrived. I was very proud that I'd been chosen for this treat and felt quite important as he beckoned me to the passenger's seat.

'See . . . I told you he'd come,' I said to the disbelieving onlookers who were convinced that the invitation was only a fantasy.

As we passed through the main gate, I saw Robert walking along the drive on his way home from school. I waved to him and the Superintendent stopped the car so that we could talk. Robert was very sad that I was abandoning him for the weekend and I felt guilty that I wanted to go.

Throughout the rest of the journey, the Superintendent questioned me about Robert . . . did we 'mess around with each other' . . . did Robert's father do it to him . . . how often and where. I was puzzled why he was so interested in my friend. While he was driving, he put his left hand down the front of my pants. This meant that he had to steer the car and change gear with the same hand and, every now and again, there wasn't a hand on the wheel. This seemed a very dangerous practice but it was the only aspect of the Superintendent's behaviour that I found alarming.

Eventually, he asked, 'Would your friend Robert like me as much as you do, Johnny?' I assured him that he would. In fact, secretly, I thought that Robert might like the Superintendent very much more than he liked his own father. When we arrived, I was taken on a conducted tour of the house, given a drink of milk and told to stay out in the yard for a little while. I felt scared because I wasn't used to going to new places and seldom had the opportunity to be alone. The Superintendent sensed my fear, patted me on the head and assured me that I would not be alone. He introduced me to his 'houseboy' Keith who told me that he had also been rescued by the Superintendent from problems at Suttor Cottage Boys' Home on the same estate. We compared notes and found that our lives were very similar. In fact, I concluded that life at Turner was preferable because the house-mother at Suttor was as violent as her husband.

'She's a real bitch,' Keith said. 'She loves using the strap and the cane and she don't care where she hurts you. And she's weird. She watches the boys when they have their baths.' That did not seem at all 'weird' to me at that time but I was to learn more about her deviant behaviour later.

Keith and I became good friends. Although he was fourteen months older than me, he was about the same build and I suppose that we were both the size of a modern day five year old. He had been orphaned as a baby and had lived in the cottages since he was four. The only difference between us was that he had the good fortune not to wet the bed. He assured me that, if I moved to Suttor Cottage, my buttocks would be beaten red raw on a daily basis. I concluded that I was lucky to live at Turner after all.

We had a great deal to talk about and it was some time before I asked Keith where he would be sleeping. Were we sharing the same bedroom?

'Don't you know why you're here?' he asked in bewilderment.

'Yes, I'm here for the weekend,' I replied.

'You mean you really don't know?'

'Know what?'

He looked uncomfortable.

'Johnny . . . has the Superintendent ever touched your diddle?'

I said that he had and went on to tell him about how I ran away to the Superintendent's house. He interrupted me with, 'Yes, I know about that. I was in the bedroom when you came. I sleep with him. I'm his boy. He told me about you but said nothing about you coming for the weekend.'

I feared that Keith might be angry or even jealous but he assured me that he was glad of my company. He then explained why I was there and what activities had been planned for me. When he finished talking, I gave a great sigh of relief and laughed.

'Is that all he expects? I have to do much worse things at Turner Cottage.'

'Well . . . so long as you've been warned,' he said. 'The Superintendent must really like you. He brings boys here from the other cottages but he's never brought one for the weekend before.' I glowed with pride.

The weekends were a 'mixed bag'. During the day, Keith and I had fun as never before. We went swimming and we went on outings into the country in the Superintendent's car. He took us with him when he visited the other Boys' Homes and there, of course, I met the five house-masters who had raped me at Turner Cottage. They recognised me and greeted me as though nothing had ever happened.

The nights were, of course, a different matter. It was the Superintendent who introduced me to the miracles of the movie camera. He mounted it on a tripod at the foot of the bed. One of us would have to rush to press the button and leap back onto the bed so that he could film himself in a threesome. He played the films back to us later and showed us other films of his earlier exploits with young boys. I often wonder what happened to those films and photographs. Did these men discard them when they were terminally ill? What happened when they had heart attacks and died suddenly? Someone must have found them! What did they do with them? Did they burn them to keep their relatives' perversions from other family members? Or are there historical archives of child porn home movies? Does someone have the photographic proof of what I am disclosing? How I wish I could get my hands on those films! I would like to present them to the child welfare authorities and say, 'Look, this is what happened to the kids in the protection of your authority'. I would be tempted to add that, however negligent my mother might have been, the harm she did me was miniscule compared with the harm inflicted by some employees of State welfare services. But would anyone be interested now? I doubt it!

The Superintendent collected me every weekend. Sometimes Robert came too. I liked that because we were a great comfort to each other when we had to do something that we didn't like.

Quite suddenly, I was discarded. I was very upset about it because there was no explanation or warning. It happened on my tenth birthday. The Superintendent failed to collect me and I racked my brains to try to work out what I'd done wrong. With hindsight, I realise that my only sin was that I'd grown taller and older and no longer met the needs of a man who only wanted little boys who looked like five year olds.

I still have very ambivalent feelings towards the Superintendent. He breached my trust and, with hindsight, was just as perverted as the other men I knew in the Cottage Homes. On the other hand, he was often kind, gentle and considerate. He never raised his voice or hit his boys. He hugged me and told me that he loved me and that I was important to him. And that was certainly important to me.

At the same time, his perversion probably made the mass abuse of children possible. When there is corruption in management, it often permeates throughout the whole of the organisation. How else can one account for the fact that so many house-parents used children for sadism and sex in one institution?

The cycle is complete

When my weekends with the Superintendent came to an end, life at the cottage returned to 'normal' and, once again, I became the prime target for the house-father's sadistic practices. As the Superintendent's 'favourite boy', I had, to some extent, been protected and Mr L had turned his attentions to two younger children. Now, he gained satisfaction from teaching me to inflict pain on others. One night, I refused to squeeze the testicles of a young boy named Tommy. I knew only too well how much it would hurt. The house-father was enraged that I dared to disobey him and he hit me with the full force of his hand across my mouth. As I keeled over, he grabbed my testicles and squeezed hard. I screamed loudly as the pain spread across my body.

'Now, you little cunt, if you don't do as you're told, I'll cut your balls off,' he said.

I had no doubt that he was capable of carrying out his threat and, thereafter, I complied with his instructions. However, 'Yes sir, I'll do it, sir' was always followed by, 'Sorry, Tommy, I have to do it'. But neither my apology nor my sympathetic glances decreased the intensity of the pain suffered by these little six and seven year olds and when they cried, I suffered too.

Robert and I were now very close. When either of us had the misfortune to be chosen as a victim for adult sexual barbarism, the other empathised. We sat for hours on the front steps and on the back verandah and we talked and talked. Mostly, we talked about escaping from our hostile world but it was not merely a matter of running away from the cottage (which we knew to be futile) but journeying to other continents. In our imaginary travels, there were no limits. We sailed around Cape Horn with the wind and the rain on our faces. We were the first conquerors of Mount Everest. We crossed deserts by camel. Wherever we went, there were only the two of us and we were always safe because there were no adults in our world.

The saddest time of my life was when Robert confided that his father was about to leave his job at the cottage. I could not believe it. Surely Robert could take me with him? The house-parent's departure should have been a time for celebration but, of course, it wasn't because he was taking his son away from me. I was distraught.

As the date of departure drew near, we spent our time together on the steps crying and consoling each other. Robert's dad was my father figure and Robert was my adopted 'brother'. Despite all that I had suffered at the hands of Mr L, this was the only family that I'd ever really known. We promised that we would maintain contact with each other for the rest of our lives.

Until the very last moment, I refused to accept the inevitable. And then the taxi arrived and Robert and his family closed the doors and the car began to move slowly along the drive. I suddenly panicked and ran after them crying, 'Stop! Please don't go. Please don't leave me. Please . . .' But the taxi picked up speed and left me behind. As I write, I can still see Robert's pale, sad face as he waved through the rear window and mouthed words that I could not hear.

For many weeks, I was in a state of total despair. I alternated between loving and missing Robert and hating him because he'd deserted me. One moment I longed for his company and the next, I denied that he meant anything to me. I was sad and I was angry but, much worse, I was alone. My world had fallen apart.

I scarcely noticed the arrival of the new house-master and it mattered little that he took his caring role seriously and never hurt or abused us. He had no wife and, with little assistance in the cottage, the older boys were given considerable responsibility for the care of younger ones, especially after school and at weekends. The kindness of the house-master was lost on the older boys. They merely perceived him as weak and they continued to prey on younger residents.

The new house-father took us out into the world to gain new experiences. Those who did not wet their beds were taken to camps. That, of course, precluded me. Some went to football matches. The most exciting day of my life was the day that we went to the Amusement Park at the Royal Easter Show. I had never seen anything like it in my life and I was mesmerised by the crowd and the different kinds of equipment. I was so fascinated by the game in which people aimed balls at the mouths of clowns' heads which moved from side to side that I failed to notice that I'd become detached from the group. I suddenly realised that I was lost and surrounded only by strangers. I had no idea what to do and, like other kids caught in such circumstances, I cried. People stopped to ask me what was wrong but I was sobbing so much that I couldn't respond. They called a policeman. He bent down to eye level and asked, 'What's wrong, son?'

I saw his uniform and felt safe. He took my hand and said, 'Come with me . . . we'll soon find your parents'.

I told him that I had no parents, that I lived at the Boys' Home and had never been anywhere like this before in my whole life.

'Have you been on the rides?' he asked.

I shook my head. 'Well, we can soon fix that,' he said. And before I knew what was happening, I was on the carousel and the bumper cars and the big wheel and he bought me candy floss and ice-cream and lollies. My head was spinning with excitement and, with the sugary combination, my stomach was beginning to feel queasy. At that point, my new friend said, 'Right, we'd better get you to the police office to wait for your house-master'.

He held my hand and smiled. I looked up apprehensively and recall thinking, 'When is he going to ask me to play around with him?' This was the first man that I ever met who gave me lollies and nice things without wanting sex. I couldn't understand it and felt apprehensive. I never knew the policeman's name but I have always cherished his memory.

On that day, I learned a valuable lesson . . . that it pays to get lost at Royal Shows; the other boys had not been on the rides. As a consequence, the following year, I managed to get lost again and had the same treats provided by a different police officer. I began to think that all police were wonderful and I would have happily set up my bed in their office at the Showground and remained there forever.

At the age of thirteen, I was promoted to the rank of 'Big boy'. This meant that I had responsibility for showering and dressing my own group of little boys. This involved the same routines that were used on me throughout childhood. I also cleaned the children's teeth and their shoes and prepared them for bed and for school. After ten years of helplessness, I now had power as my right. The older boys felt that they had 'earned' this power through their own years of victimisation. It was an institutionalised rite of passage but, nevertheless, I found it hard to grasp that these young boys would do anything . . . absolutely anything that I demanded of them. There was no adult supervision in the bathroom and all the boys were naked together. As before, the big boys initiated genital touching and the boys who had reached puberty had competitions to see who could ejaculate first.

I am as guilty as hell for abusing my own group of boys. After ten years of learning, it never occurred to me that the method of showering was wrong and could be conducted differently. It may sound like a lame excuse but I would have been derided and further abused if I hadn't joined in. But there are four things that I firmly refused to do to anyone else: I would never engage in anal sex; I would never involve children in licking; I would never insert foreign objects into their bodies; and I would never make children drink noxious fluids. And I have kept those rules throughout my life because I have never recovered from the pain of my own experiences and probably never will.

My last two years at Turner Cottage continued in much the same way as before except for two things; I was never belted for bedwetting and I was never abused (in any way) by the new house-father. I was still sexually abused by the older boys but I did not view it as harmful and, much of the time, I liked what they did. This was the only approval that I ever received and, at this stage, I would even tolerate the obnoxious and the painful for that attention.

Berry Boys' Home

One day, a welfare officer arrived, packed my few possessions and took me for a train ride. I was going to Berry Home to join the older boys. I was absolutely fascinated as we passed through dairy country and I saw my first cow! And when we arrived at our destination, I was puzzled by the large sign posted at the entrance, 'Berry Husbandry School'. I knew what berries were and I expected to continue my schooling (having reached only fifth grade in primary school) but 'husbandry' had me completely baffled. I knew what a husband was (or thought I did) and I assumed that I was about to be trained as one.

Berry Boys' Home had big gates and a long drive leading up to a substantial property. At the front of the house was a garden and fountain encircled by the driveway. I looked around and liked what I saw: there was a cricket pitch in a paddock behind a small cottage and a sense of spaciousness everywhere.

I was taken to the office for formalities to be completed. Then, the man said that I must meet the Superintendent. We walked along the verandah to his office. The man knocked, waited for a response and ushered me inside. I looked around and, behind a huge, impressive desk was the former Superintendent from Mittagong . . . yes, the man with whom I had spent my weekends. He was the last person on earth that I expected to see there and I greeted him like a long lost father. He recognised me immediately, eyed me up and down with a look of approval and commented that I'd grown. Nonetheless I was still only as tall as the average seven year old and he had no difficulty in picking me up and sitting me on his knee. He dismissed the clerk and told him to close the door. And when we were alone, my new Superintendent kissed me on the head and whispered, 'I've missed you Johnny'.

I still had strong feelings for this man because my recollections of him were those associated with gentleness and kindness. Nevertheless, I suspected insincerity; he had dismissed me arbitrarily on my tenth birthday, hurt my feelings and provided no explanation for the rejection. Why, if he missed me, did he discard me?

I plucked up the courage to ask him that question. He just smiled and responded, 'I had to'. There was no opportunity to press for a more sensible explanation because his hands were already fondling me. The Superintendent kept me in his office for more than half an hour and I will spare you the details. At the end, he showed me the layout of the building and warned me that I would be troubled by the sixteen and seventeen-year-old boys who lived at Berry Boys' Home. He said that he would protect me and all I had to do was report problems to him. Little did he realise how much power he was giving me.

I was pleased to find that I already knew most of the residents. They had lived at Waverley or Turner Cottages at some time or other and it was like being reunited with my extended family. I was given work on the dairy farm and had to milk the cows and clean the shed. I had no more schooling because I was considered to be 'too old at fourteen' to attend Nowra Secondary School. There was no agricultural education at the Home either; we were merely labourers doing the menial tasks on the farm.

Altogether, we had a staff of twelve including two house-fathers and their wives, a cook, a head farm manager, a head dairy manager and four assistants. And, of course, the Superintendent. Of these twelve people, only two involved the boys in sexual behaviour: the Superintendent and the dairy man. I first encountered *him* when I was asked to take something to the calf shed and I caught him red-handed with one of the boys. The boy was petrified that I might 'dob him in' which I found remarkable given that he was older and bigger than me. He warned me that the man had sex with lots of boys and was known for his brutality.

'Why do you put up with it?' I asked. 'Why don't you tell the Super?'

He replied, 'No-one would believe me'.

I was suddenly reminded of my own attempts at disclosure and replied, 'Maybe you're right'.

'Don't let him catch you on your own,' the lad said but, of course, I took no notice of the warning because I was convinced that I was under the protection of the Superintendent. Four days later, on a Saturday afternoon, I was trying to stack hay in the hayshed and as I gave one big, final push, I sensed the presence of someone behind me. I turned quickly and found myself in a vice-like grip.

'Having trouble are we Johnny?' I tried to wriggle out of the dairy man's arms.

'Don't do that Johnny, you know you like it.' He was wrong, I hated it. I hated him and I hated his smell and I fought back but I lost.

'If you don't let me go, I'll scream my head off,' I threatened.

'Have a look up there,' he said, referring to the stacked bales of hay. 'If they fell down on you, no-one would find you for ages. Poor Johnny! He's had an accident.'

I knew that it would be the easiest thing in the world for this tough individual to send all the bales down on top of me. I wasn't prepared to take that risk and I stopped fighting. He raped me and I was in agony but worse, I felt filthy. He was the first man that I really hated . . . I mean hated so much that I wanted to see him dead. But unlike the other boys I knew that I had some control over what was happening. I reported him to the Superintendent.

'You're not working at the dairy farm any more,' he said.

'But sir . . . I like it there.'

He smiled. 'Yes, I know you do but I want to keep an eye on you. I want you here with me.'

'But you haven't got a houseboy, sir.'

'I have one now,' he said and patted me reassuringly.

I expected that the dairy man would be fired and that the Superintendent would take action to protect the other boys but he did nothing to help them. Only I was protected. I had the last laugh when the man's tractor overturned and he suffered fatal injuries. I recall thinking that there was some justice in the world after all and God *was* on our side; the man was dead and we were alive. My

91

hatred departed when all the boys were forced to go through the pretence of mourning him at his funeral. I refused to go and my refusal was accepted. I felt vindicated.

The Big Boy system at Berry was quite different to any other; it was size and not age related. The big boys ruled the home. They were often younger than me but they were thugs and operated in cliques. With the safety of group support, they did things that they would not dare do when unaccompanied . . . and that included raping anyone they fancied, or anyone they wished to demean. I saw young boys being attacked and pack raped by groups of six or seven thugs. No-one ever intervened. They were never reported because there was a strong code of silence. Most of the victims had been reared in boys' homes where they had to tolerate anything to amuse their depraved house-masters and they accepted it as part of their lot in life. Because we could do little to stop it, we shrugged it off. By virtue of its very frequency at Berry, rape was no big deal.

I made friends with two boys, Eric and Allen. We had adjacent beds and participated in sexual activities which were mutual and private. The three of us used to walk to church together but, on one occasion, I ran ahead and climbed a tree . . . intending to take them by surprise. I was the one who received the surprise because, as I bent over to call to them, the branch broke off and I fell head first to the ground. I was stunned temporarily but picked myself up and went into church with the others. I recall singing the first verse of 'Rock of ages cleft for me' and, when I next opened my eyes I was lying on the Minister's bed being stroked by a new 'relief' house-master who had one hand on my cheek and the other down the front of my pants. When I sat up, he calmly said, 'You had a nasty bump on your head, Johnny. We're taking you back home in the Minister's car.'

When we returned to the house, the building was in darkness and the boys were asleep. The new house-master undressed me, put on my pyjamas and lifted me into bed. The next morning, Eric explained that I'd collapsed in church and struck my head on the corner of the pew. This, combined with the fall from the tree, had caused concussion and I'd been in the Minister's bed for several hours.

I learned that the new, temporary house-master had picked me up and carried me from the church and that he was by my side throughout the evening. I told Eric about finding his hand in my pants.

'Are you going to tell the Super?' Eric asked.

'I don't think so,' I said. 'He didn't hurt. And he was kind.'

'Will you let him do it again?' asked Eric, assuming that the Super's special boy would have a choice.

'I don't know,' I mused. 'I'll have to think about it. I'll see how things go.'

At the end of the day, I was sitting alone on the steps of the house when the house-master squatted down beside me.

'How are you feeling? You've got a beaut bump on your head but then you gave it a mighty whack. Do you remember anything about last night?'

'I climbed a tree and the branch broke off,' I said.

'No, not that . . . later . . . when you woke up. Do you remember what I was doing?'

'Yes, sir.'

'And it doesn't worry you?'

'No, sir.'

He breathed a sigh of relief, patted me approvingly, stood up and said, 'The Super was right. You are a loving boy.'

I thought about this statement carefully and concluded that if the Superintendent had told him about me, the man must be trustworthy. And when he asked me which children were orphans, which had no visitors and which kids liked to 'fool around', I gave him their names. I knew that he could have searched the records for himself but, of course, it never occurred to me that a search by a temporary staff member might have attracted the suspicions of other staff. Unwittingly, I provided him with all the information that he needed to create his own group of 'favourite boys' and, of course, I was one of them.

We were all very suspicious of him because he was different to the other house-masters. We thought it strange that he never involved more than one boy at a time. Furthermore, he never did anything without asking our permission. He was a gentle man in every way and I liked his company. He often talked about his wartime experiences and showed me photographs of the places that he'd visited. And sometimes he showed me pornography; sex always followed. He, in common with the earlier house-masters, was a capable photographer and took his own collection of pornographic photographs involving me. But he was quiet, non-violent and 'considerate' and that, in my value system, made him a 'nice man'.

The house-master had only a short-term contract and he left

after three months. The Superintendent was on holiday and with both protectors gone, the older boys gave us a very hard time.

My friends Eric and Owen were tricked into entering the hay shed where they were subjected to a vicious beating and sexual degradation at the hands of the bigger boys. Allan was also raped and degraded by six of them while Eric and I were held down and forced to watch. And all of the time, the pack jeered that our 'Mother hen' was no longer there to protect us and we deserved all that was coming. What happened to those two boys should never have happened to anyone. I had seen and experienced some terrible things in my life but nothing so horrendous as was inflicted by this group of thugs on their own peers. When they finished with Allen, they surrounded me.

Victor, the leader, bent down, looked me directly in the eye and said, 'Now, it's your turn, little shit'. He pulled my pants down, grabbed my buttocks, laughed and said, 'But not today. I'll save you for another day.' He then kicked Allan in the kidneys and I saw red. I don't know where I found the strength but the two boys who had been pinning me down released their hold and I exploded, flinging myself at Victor. Despite the impediment of my shorts being around my ankles, I gave him all that I had. I didn't care that Victor and his cronies had the capacity to hurt me more than I could ever hurt them. I'd had enough and I wanted to hurt him badly . . . regardless of the price I would have to pay.

What happened next took me completely by surprise. Two of my punches landed accurately and Victor, almost twice my size, suddenly began to cry, protesting that I was hurting him. I was disgusted by his whining and ignored his plea to stop. 'I'm sorry. I promise I won't do it again,' he said. His supporters backed off. 'He's chicken', one said and they all agreed. They abandoned him to me and my friends.

'What shall we do with him?' they asked.

'Nothing,' I replied in disgust. 'He isn't worth it.'

We picked Allan up, showered him and put him to bed. He never recovered from that terrible attack. Allan had been a bright kid who had done well at school but, on that day, he lost interest in everything and he was never the same again.

When the Superintendent returned, I reported what had happened and the ten boys concerned were transferred to other Boys' Homes. A new house-master arrived and with a lovely wife and son, the atmosphere of the home began to change. It was impossible for them to stop the sexual activities of the boys and they punished those caught masturbating or molesting others. The house-parents lived in separate quarters, however, and they could not supervise us closely. As a consequence, the older boys continued to abuse the young with little fear of being caught.

The house-parents' son, Sean, spent a lot of time with us and I got to know him very well. One day, we got into conversation about sex. It happened very innocently when I saw that he had white fabric under his pants and learned that they were underpants. I enquired what they were for and he said that his mother made them. Out of the blue, he asked me whether the boys played with each other. I cautiously asked what he meant.

'You know . . . play with their doodles,' he said.

'Some of them do,' I replied. 'Why do you want to know?'

He said that his father disapproved of masturbation and punished him for it because it was 'dirty'. I was puzzled because no-one had referred to it as 'dirty' before. What was 'dirty' about it? We knew that his father punished boys for doing it but 'dirty' . . .? It seemed a strange thing to say. Sean revealed that he had been sexually abused by an instructor at another institution where his father previously worked. He described it as a 'big home in Sydney'.

'Yashmar?' I asked.

'Do you know it?'

'Yashmar has a terrible reputation.'

Sean revealed that staff and older boys had abused him not just at Yashmar but at all the cottage homes where his father had worked. Sean told no-one about it because the staff swore him to secrecy. I suddenly realised that he had been abused almost as frequently as the other boys and he, like Robert before him, was a house-master's son, not a ward of the State. That convinced me more than ever that kids were abused everywhere, regardless of their status. After that, Sean and I became inseparable friends. I remained at Berry Boys' Home until I was nineteen. Throughout that time, I continued to provide sex for the Superintendent and he, in return, provided protection for me.

Facing the world outside

I left the care of the State to join the army. Then, a whole new terrifying world suddenly opened up. For the first time in my life I was surrounded by adults instead of boys.

I was inadequately educated and virtually illiterate. I didn't know how to behave in adult company and I knew absolutely nothing about the female gender. At that stage, I had never met any girls, least of all had practice in relating to them. My sex education was exclusively that taught by adult male paedophiles in welfare homes.

An old 'Digger' saw my predicament and took me under his wing, helping me to read and write. But when the other men talked about their sexual exploits I had no idea what they were talking about and dare not disclose my ignorance. And when I was based in Malaya and my peers persuaded me to accompany them to a brothel in Malacca, I went willingly because I had no idea what a brothel was (and dare not ask).

As we entered the chosen house, a woman enquired whether I would like a 'giggy gig'. Not knowing what a giggy gig involved, I looked dubious and my companions answered for me. I was then guided to a room in which there was little furniture other than a double bed. As my eyes became accustomed to the dim light, I was shocked to see a naked woman sitting on the bed. I'd never seen a woman's body before and I took fright. As she stood up to greet me, my eyes automatically turned to her groin. I couldn't believe what I saw. She'd lost her genitals!

I was convinced that I was in the presence of a freak and ran out of the house as fast as I could. Two weeks went by before I revealed my plight to my Digger friend and he sat me down and explained the facts of life. The trouble was that it all sounded very unattractive and unnatural. After sixteen years of sex with boys and house-masters, I wasn't remotely interested in finding out about sex with girls; it scared me to death. With my sexual leanings so well entrenched, I began to find that I was emotionally, socially and sexually crippled . . . a misfit in adult society. I knew for certain that I wasn't sexually attracted to other men. I had a couple of homosexual experiences with soldiers and found them revolting. I'd had more than enough of men's sexual demands in the boys' homes. But I was equally repulsed by the thought of sex with a woman. In other words, I was isolated.

When I joined the Army, I began to do what I'd been forbidden to do at Berry . . . I started a search to track down my old friend, Robert. Eventually, I located his grandmother in Sydney and I decided to call on her when I was on leave. She wasn't expecting me and I was relieved when I heard someone coming to answer the door. The door opened and there, to my amazement, was Robert. At first we just stared at each other in stunned amazement.

Then we embraced, tears streaming down our cheeks. And then, of course, we talked . . . and talked.

Robert had joined the Air Force and, by a remarkable coincidence, we found that we were based only a few miles apart. We saw each other frequently from then onwards and, if anything, our affection and friendship deepened. Our love was truly a brotherly, trusting love in which there was no hint of sexual contact. Robert, like me, never married and our bond continued until he met his untimely death in a car accident a few years ago. That was the worst part of my life because, when Robert died, I sensed that part of me died with him.

I survived Army life, probably because it was, in many ways, like the institutional life with which I was familiar. You did as you were told. You were not expected to think for yourself. And if you were taught that 2+2=16, that is what you had to believe. You couldn't complain. And you had to trust those in command. Both the Army and the children's homes dictated every aspect of your life. There was only one obvious difference; the children's homes rationed you to one piece of toilet paper per visit; the Army was a little more generous.

In the meantime, I realised that I was different to other men and I didn't much like what I'd become. I sought help from two different psychologists both of whom revealed their revulsion when I disclosed my sexual leanings. I had long accepted responsibility for the fact that I had been abused . . . 'It must have been my own fault . . . I must have "asked for it" . . . it was my fault for wetting the bed (etc)'. I felt like dirt and lacked the courage to return for more therapy. I sensed that no-one understood and I had to try to tackle the problem by myself. I couldn't talk to my friends about it because I was scared that they would reject me too. I was still searching for love, as I had in childhood, but I didn't even know what love really was or why it was so important to me.

Where could I go for help? There were support groups for alcoholics, drug addicts, gamblers and even smokers. My addiction was even more of a problem to society but no-one really wanted to know about it.

When I completed my Army service, I met and formed a sexual relationship with a fourteen-year-old boy. I thought that I loved him. All went well until we were caught fondling each other. We were both charged with committing acts of indecency. I pleaded guilty in court and I received a nine month jail sentence. This came as a tremendous shock because, until that moment, I had not realised that what I was doing constituted a serious crime. I became totally confused and had to re-think everything that I had been taught in childhood. It was a very traumatic period.

I was sent to Long Bay Jail in Sydney where I was put to work in the pantry which adjoins No. 8 yard. One afternoon, I was standing outside the pantry when I saw a familiar face on the other side of the fence. I called out 'Wayne' and the man looked up. He came towards me and I realised that he didn't recognise me.

'Do you know me?' he asked.

'Do I know you? Of course I do! How could I forget you? Hold on and I'll get 'the screw' to let you in so that we can have a talk.'

I knew that I'd changed a lot since leaving Berry Boys' Home. I was no longer undersized and underweight; twelve years in the Army had contributed substantially to my physique. I'd thickened out and I was then very fit.

The prisoner joined me and we sat together on a bench.

'Remember me? . . . I'm Johnny,' I said.

I could see that he was having difficulty in placing me.

'Think back . . . to Waverley Cottage,' I said, but there was still a blank expression on his face.

'You should remember me, you bastard. I'm the kid you forced to drink three bottles full of piss . . . your piss.'

He became tense.

'You're not him!' he said with an air of disbelief. 'You're having me on . . . You're not Little Johnny.'

Child molesters seldom imagine that their victims will, one day, grow up and think badly of them. Until they are in jail, it doesn't occur to them that someone may be waiting for an opportunity for revenge. All the terrible things that Wayne had done to me came flooding back . . . only now, the tables were reversed and I was in control. He fidgeted nervously.

I'm not a violent man but I admit that I set out to hurt Wayne. I succeeded. He ended up with a broken nose, a fractured jaw and a couple of cracked ribs. I was charged with assault . . . which, of course, I expected . . . but the charges were dropped when I explained why I'd hurt him. I had, without realising it, carried so much hatred around with me for so many years that, when it was all over, I felt a tremendous sense of relief.

There was no Assessment and Therapy Programme for sex offenders at Long Bay Jail and I emerged feeling more helpless and hopeless than ever. I went 'bush' to avoid people but, eventually,

I met another youth and found myself in exactly the same situation as before.

It was only when I came to prison for the second time that my problems were taken seriously. At long last, someone was prepared to listen without sitting in judgment. Gradually, with help, I began to understand myself and why I am the way I am. A heavy load was lifted from my shoulders when I was prescribed Depro Provera . . . a suppressant which helps to control my deviant thoughts and dreams. When I left Berry Boys' Home, I didn't suddenly stop seeing boys as sex objects. Sixteen years of learning could not be undone overnight just because I'd moved into a different world. I'd been steeped in a deviant, obsessive, sexual environment and I remained obsessed when I left. I hated myself and my life but only when I joined the prison programme could I disclose my problems openly and honestly. I then decided to 'wipe the slate clean' and admit offences with two other boys which had not previously been disclosed. I again pleaded guilty in court and received a long sentence. I was actually pleased because it meant that I will have a much better chance of making the necessary changes before release.

What happened to me in the Boys' Homes was not at all unusual. There are at least four ex-Mittagong residents in this small prison community, three of whom committed murders. Our combined experiences of that boys' home span more than thirty years. During that time, we all suffered the same kinds of abuse at the hands of the same and different people. A Brisbane organisation, Formerly in Children's Homes (FICH) claims that more than 250 000 living Australians were sexually, physically and emotionally brutalised while in the care of the State, the churches and the Salvation Army.

It worries me that I perpetuated the abuse cycle and may have damaged other lives. It worries me that my victims could become the next generation of child molesters. I pray to God that, somehow, those boys might escape and lead normal lives. But, sadly, God's record of success in child protection leaves a lot to be desired.

The question is, what can ordinary humans do to prevent history from repeating itself?

5

Little Jim

'Little Jim is a misfit, a misfit, a misfit.'

'He's the fat one . . . the ugly one . . . the one with the big nose. Haven't you noticed that his eyes are crooked? As for his ears . . . they're as big as an elephant's. And you could fit a football in his mouth!'

'Little Jim is clumsy and stupid. He can't do anything right. No-one knows who he takes after. It can't be our side of the family. He's different to the others . . . definitely the odd one out.'

'The worst thing is that he's sex-mad. He's always taking his clothes off in public. He's been doing it for most of his life. Our worst fear is that he'll grow up to be one of those poofters. He's definitely odd.'

Little Jim knows how his parents perceive him. They never miss an opportunity to remind him of his shortcomings. His Dad calls him 'the log' because 'he's thick and has no brains'.

Little Jim's mother thought that she'd protected her sons from the risk of sexual abuse when she told them to avoid being kidnapped by dangerous strangers: 'Never talk to dirty old men, never accept money from dirty old men, never accept lollies, never get in a car with a stranger'. At the age of five, little Jim didn't know what a stranger was but he felt sure that he would recognise one instantly if he saw one. In the meantime, his mother did nothing to protect him from sexual abuse by his father, his two brothers, relatives, school teachers, a clergyman and his dad's best mates. Little Jim was sexually abused by no less than ten different offenders in the first few years of his life. Nine of them were relatives and trusted family friends. Although it didn't feel quite right, it was not until many years later that it dawned on Jim that what they did was wrong.

Little Jim is now concealed inside a six foot tall, powerfully built forty-eight-year-old body. Big Jim has a family of his own. He has been successful in business and pretends to be the life and soul of the party. But delve just a little beneath that outgoing veneer and you find a confused and frightened little boy who still needs the approval of his long dead father, whose sexuality has been irrevocably damaged and whose sadness is overwhelming.

When I volunteered to write about my early childhood experiences, I suddenly realised that I had never had the opportunity to be a child. My very first memory involves being used for oral sex. I am a baby and I'm wearing a nappy. I can see the lower half of a man. My face is level with the opening in his pants. I recognise the trousers: I've seen them lots of times. They belong to my father. I have a sore throat and feel that I'm about to choke. This scene appears again and again in my adult nightmares and the choking feeling returns.

My second memory is crystal clear. It involves my half-brother who is fourteen years older than me. Jeff and I share the same bedroom and he takes me into his bed when I have bad dreams. I have them often. He cuddles me and comforts me and I love him. This is the only positive attention that I receive as a child and he makes me feel wanted. I rush into his bed when I waken in the morning and, when the cuddles are especially good, I reward him by sliding down the sheets to suck his penis. I don't know why but I do this spontaneously: I associate this with wanting to please him. There is no sense of coercion, no threat, no force, no trickery . . . he doesn't ask me to do it, I take the initiative and do this of my own volition. I know what I'm doing, where I'm going and why . . . and I am not yet two years old.

This happened regularly and I have never been able to forget that I, a toddler, initiated sex. This has haunted me throughout my life, convincing me that I was sexually deviant from birth . . . a worthless, evil child, just as my mother had proclaimed.

'Maybe your half-brother taught you what to do and you forgot' suggested my therapist, trying to be helpful. 'After all, you were less than two years old.'

No, my half-brother wasn't responsible. Of all my childhood memories, this is far and away the clearest. When, many years later, I was able to mention the subject to Jeff, he confirmed that my recollections were correct and he admitted to being puzzled by my early sexual awareness. For most of my life I could tell no-one of my dark secret because I carried so much guilt, self-hatred and recrimination. This set a pattern of timidity and fear. I was afraid of everything and everyone. Scratch the confident mask and the fear is still there.

My next recollection of sexual abuse again involves oral rape by my father. I was about five years old. I am sure that this happened in the stable because, whenever I think about it, I experience the powerful smell of straw and horses.

I am in no doubt that my father used me for sex over a very long period of time but the memories are hazy and so painful that I have buried the detail at the back of my mind. I don't want to remember because I can't cope with it. I underwent a whole year of therapy before I found the courage to say that my dad abused me in infancy. And so I move on to my mother . . .

My mother always felt that she had 'married beneath her social station' and 'deserved better' than my father. She had already had an illegitimate son to someone else when she married him. Together, they concealed the truth by writing false dates on their own wedding photographs to deceive their children in later years. Having concocted their secret, they were stuck with it and we (unwittingly) celebrated their silver wedding and bought them gifts several years before the anniversary indicated by the date on their marriage certificate.

When, after their deaths, I learned of the deception, I realised that my parents had been deceiving each other throughout their married lives, often using their sons as pawns and keepers of their secrets.

My father persuaded my brothers to invest their hard-earned savings in successive business ventures. They dared not refuse. One of my brothers was only sixteen years old but he had pretended to be much older for employment purposes and, when involved in an accident, received the compensation due to an adult. My father took it all. When his businesses were successful, my father sold them and kept their money. He confided in me but instructed me to keep it secret. I accidentally revealed the sale to my brothers. That created an uproar in the family and I suffered a severe whipping as punishment for my indiscretion.

My father was a race horse trainer who owned his own stables on the outskirts of Melbourne. His work necessitated leaving home early each morning. He went to bed early each night and spent the remainder of his day at the pub. He had very little contact with my mother but always impressed upon his children that they had an obligation to protect her. She was very capable of taking care of herself and did so whenever it suited her but, together, they used her deficient eyesight to impose on their sons, treating us like guide-dogs who had no rights and whose sole purpose in life was to serve her.

My parents had little in common, other than their disapproval of me. My mother was teetotal and hated alcohol. My father drank heavily and often came home drunk. He was always looking for an opportunity to argue and fight and the tension was unbearable. My mother was hard, mean and hyper-critical. There was no element of joy or warmth in our relationship. She criticised meanness in other relatives without realising that she was the meanest of them all. Her only aim in life was to have a spotlessly clean house with 'a place for everything and everything in its place'.

She demanded to be protected by her children but I find it hard to think of anything positive that she did to protect them. She controlled my brothers by reminding them of her disability and, being the youngest, I watched and identified her modus operandi. I decided, at a very early age, that I wanted to remain at a distance from her, I never liked her and, as I grew older, I even hated her. Again, this made me feel terribly guilty because boys and men are supposed to love their mothers. I felt that there was something wrong with me and I only managed to reveal my hatred after months in therapy.

To the best of my knowledge, my brother never told me to keep the oral sex secret from my parents but I knew that this was necessary. Jeff warned me that I must try to stop talking in my sleep because my mother 'spied' on me and came into the bedroom when I had nightmares . . . which was almost nightly. To stay safe, I had to try to stay awake and bedtime became a time of great anxiety.

As I grew older, I regarded my mother as 'smutty' and embarrassing because she was always looking for sexual connotations to innocent situations. Soon after I started school, I lost a sock after a dancing session. Little boys often lose school clothing, especially clothing that is unmarked. My mother was so suspicious that she reported the loss to my father. He cross examined me and beat me with his riding crop for a full half-hour. 'Who were you with? Why did you take your clothes off? Who else was there? What else did you take off? Where did you go? You'd better tell me the truth because I'm going to go round to that school and find out for myself!'

The extent of my father's hypocrisy only became apparent much later. Shortly afterwards, an older cousin came to stay with us and, because the house was full, I had to share his double bed. His family lived in the country but he was forced to come to the city to find work. He was fourteen and I was six. I have very vivid memories of going to bed with him. He involved me in sexual activity from the very first day. At first, it was fun, it felt good and I liked the attention. I was too young to notice that he only gave me that attention when he wanted me for sex.

Soon, he became dissatisfied with genital touching and masturbation and demanded anal sex. At this point, I began to detach my mind from my body so that I felt no pain and could shut the memories out. In my nightmares, my body remained in the bed while I floated above it, observing everything that happened to little Jim but feeling nothing. These nightmares have persisted throughout my life. The sexual abuse occurred daily and only stopped when I refused to provide oral sex and, at about the same time, my cousin found a girlfriend.

I did not tell my mother about what was happening because my cousin had already made it clear that she would not believe me. 'And, even if she believes you, she'll say it's your own fault and she'll go stark raving mad,' he said. And I knew that he was right.

At about the same time, my second brother, John, anally raped me. He was then sixteen and I was six. He had used the bathroom and I was surprised when he came into my bedroom . . . stark naked and sexually aroused. He said that he wanted to show me something. He told me to strip off my clothes and bend over the bed. The next moment, he was trying to rape me. This gave me a painful, burning, tearing sensation and I yelled at him to stop. He said, 'Relax. It won't hurt', but I couldn't relax and it hurt like hell. I cried out again. He said, 'Just be patient. It will get better. You'll learn to like it.'

I told him that I hated it and continued yelling until he stopped. I can remember no more except that my brother attempted to have anal sex whenever he managed to get me alone. He succeeded in penetrating me on four occasions but never with the success that he wanted because it always caused me enormous pain.

On the fourth occasion, he bribed me with ten shillings to let him 'try again'. Ten shillings was a great deal of money for a six year old and it was hard to resist the offer but the result was no better than before. By now, I was afraid of my brother. I could not understand why he wanted to hurt me. At the same time, I felt terribly guilty and dishonest because I accepted the ten shillings but failed to give him what he wanted. I felt anxious because I wanted and needed and felt that it was my responsibility to please him. Strange as it may seem, the guilt surrounding my indebtedness to my brother accompanied me into adulthood.

When he could not get anal sex from me, my brother demanded oral sex. I now found this obnoxious. I had learned something about hygiene and didn't want to put germs in my mouth from the thing he used for 'peeing'.

In the meantime, my parents were beginning to worry about my overt sexual behaviour and suspected that I was involved with deviant older boys outside the home. It never occurred to them that I was being abused by my own brother. They increased my vulnerability to sexual abuse by making him chaperone me wherever I went. He took me to school. He came to the playground to 'check up' on me at lunchtime. He took me to the cinema and the theatre and he was outraged when a man in the next seat put his hands up my pants.

One day, while walking home from the swimming pool, my brother left the path and called me over to look inside a large concrete sewage pipe on a building site adjacent to the Town Hall. 'Come here. I want to show you something. There are jewels in this pipe,' he said. I believed him and followed, only to find that his jewels were his genitals and he wanted oral sex. That was too much for me and I ran home.

My fear of John increased and I used to hide from him in the wardrobe to avoid his aggressive sexual attentions. It was dark and uncomfortable and I found it difficult to breathe but I would stay there for half an hour or more until I was sure that he had left the house or someone else had arrived home. My mother knew that I hid but she regarded this as further proof of my weirdness.

Primary school was a highly sexual environment for boys. Unsupervised by teaching staff, open school urinals facilitated frequent mutual touching, sexual curiosity, exploration, the comparison of genital size and, of course, competition relating to who could urinate higher or further than anyone else. 'Dirty talk' flourished and children were excited by it because they knew that if teachers heard, they would be outraged. We all knew that adults behaved rudely with each other but we also knew that they liked to keep rude behaviour to themselves.

I had first-hand knowledge of deviant sex while most boys were still fascinated by faeces and 'lavatory words'. This knowledge was in great demand and I achieved considerable popularity as unofficial teacher and demonstrator in peer group sex education. This made no mention of females and babies of course.

My obsession with sex quickly brought me into contact with older boys who were, in effect, adolescent sex offenders. In me, they found a willing victim for their activities and, at first, I felt important and privileged to be invited to join in this comparatively mature and experienced social group. They took me to empty buildings to participate in sexual conversation and mutual mastur-bation. Initially, I enjoyed it and went looking for them when I was bored and had nothing to do. I felt wanted, valued and, at the same time, cheap.

By the time I was seven, I knew exactly which boys were involved with sex and which were not. By the time I was nine, I had become dissatisfied with their crude behaviour because it failed to provide the emotional satisfaction and comfort that I needed. They often ignored me or belittled me in public while they used me for their own sexual gratification in private. Affection starved, I began to look towards more mature males who could act as father replacement figures. I was raped by my father's friend who gave me a lift home in his truck. He warned me not to tell my mother because 'Who would she believe . . . you or me? And even if she believed the word of an eight year old against that of her husband's best mate, she'd go mad with you. You've heard what she says . . . "If something happens to boys, it's their own stupid fault. They must have done something to deserve it!" Remember?'

Yes, I remembered it well.

My mother became increasingly suspicious of the company I kept and constantly questioned me about where I was going, where I'd been, who was there and what we did. Her method of child protection was to mount a campaign of terror to warn me of the dangers of 'poofters' and a named youth she'd 'heard about' who 'takes boys in the park and puts his dick up their bums'. My father and brothers were present throughout these tirades, dad usually hiding behind his newspaper.

I promised mum faithfully that I would never go near that dangerous park and I kept that promise but I went out looking for the youth the very next day.

My mother's hatred for homosexuals became more and more obvious. One day, she would declare that these evil perverts should be 'lined up and shot'. Another day, 'they should castrate the lot of them'. At times, she wished that 'they'd lock them all up and throw away the key'. She declared that homosexuals were responsible for raping boys. She told me of terrible things that happened to 'poofters' in jail at the hands of 'real men'. I did not fully understand what she was talking about but understood enough to realise that my mother suspected me of becoming one of these monsters.

Not surprisingly, my mother's regular pronouncements on the evils of homosexuality began to have an impact on me. She declared, openly, that I was effeminate . . . girlish . . . just like a pansy and too sensitive by far. I was constantly told how 'real men' should behave. We had a family outing on the beach when I was about eleven years old. My cousins were playing football and urged me to join in. I wanted to continue reading my book. My mother belted me with a sandal and said, 'You're joining in. Now! . . . Go on! I don't want a cissy for a son. You have to do things with the boys.' This further alienated me from my mother.

I became increasingly worried about my 'poofter' image and prison future, suffered asthma attacks, migraines and threw up every morning before I went to school. I was a nervous wreck.

Eventually, my mother managed to convince me (without realising what she had done) that, yes, I was a dreaded 'poofter' and that implied, by my mother's definition, that I was destined to become a child molester. I was totally confused by her ravings because, while I was surrounded by men who had raped me . . . (my father, my brothers, my cousin, the jockey and dad's best friends) . . . my mother perceived them as 'real men', ideal male models . . . the kind of men I should emulate.

To whom could I turn in this confusion? Certainly not my relatives or my father's friends. The only people who were likely to listen and understand were the men who liked and sympathised with young boys.

The 'dirty old men' about whom I had been warned were a figment of my mother's imagination. The real life paedophiles presented themselves as well-educated, well-dressed professionals who showed a genuine interest in me and my problems. It never occurred to me that these were the supposedly 'dangerous strangers' featured in my mother's warnings. They were clergymen and teachers and youth leaders. They were charming, friendly, concerned and generous people who treated me with more respect and consideration than I had ever received at the hands of my relatives. I was blissfully unaware of their motivation and, childlike, I accepted them at face value, attracted by the promise of a rewarding parent replacement relationship. Of course they used me for sex but so did my relatives. The difference was that, while my father, his best friend, my brother and cousin had used me as a rubber doll . . . an unfeeling, inhuman object to feed their greedy sexual appetites, paedophiles offered some kindness, consideration and compassion . . . especially in the early stages. And while my relatives discarded and rejected me instantly after they had achieved sexual gratification, paedophiles offered companionship and generosity. They were my friends. They were highly skilled seducers. They listened to me. They didn't make fun of me. They didn't regard me as different, useless, stupid or ugly. They accepted me as I was. They boosted my ego and they empathised. They were irresistible. They had the ability to communicate at my level when I was only seven, eight and nine years old and this skill is something that my parents (and most others) lacked.

I was, of course, sexually curious in an obsessive way. I could not ask my parents about sexual matters because the human body was a taboo subject. I picked up information from other boys but much of it was sensationalised and contradictory. Young boys need help to separate fact from fiction. They want to know about sexual intercourse, homosexuals, what sex is about, what people do, what it feels like. But how can parents explain what homosexuals do when they have never experienced a homosexual relationship or, worse, they believe that homosexuals are just dirty, evil deviants who should be shot?

In marked contrast, the paedophiles answered my questions openly and honestly, albeit with demonstrations and pornographic pictures to engender sexual excitement as part of the seduction process.

Boys are flattered by the special attention that these men give and they become alive. They show off their achievements and their physical prowess, 'Watch me, see how high I can swing . . . see what I can do with my bike . . . look what I've learned to do on my skateboard'. The paedophile does not say, 'Sorry, not now dear, I haven't got time . . . I'm too busy . . . come on, hurry up . . . stop being silly . . . you'll hurt yourself'. The paedophile listens, watches, admires, approves, flatters and boosts the child's ego as it has never been boosted before. And although he is a master of insincerity, children are incapable of assessing adult motives.

Starved of affection and attention at home, I became 'hooked' on this attention and embarked on sexual encounter after sexual encounter to fill the emotional void in my life. I was certain that my desire to be cuddled, hugged and touched was abnormal. In common with most of my peers, I had been conditioned by my parents, teachers and society in general to believe that boys do not need affection. I fear that this still exists. Even if parents adopt a liberal approach in the home, allow their sons to cry and take dolls to bed, the rest of society makes no similar concessions. Double standards often exist whereby parents pay lip-service to modern values at home but expect boys to conform to society's expectations in school and on the sports field. The result is confusion.

I felt weak and effeminate when I went in search of affection. I felt even weaker when I realised that I was trading sex to fulfil my emotional needs. The realisation did not stop my search; I was addicted.

By the time I was nine, I had developed the seduction process to an art form. I had my own routine of sexual innuendos which paedophiles and pederasts instantly recognised as a sign of my sexual experience and interest. I didn't much care for the sexual contact but I was addicted to all that went with it . . . the sex talk, the fatherly interest, the kindness, the gentleness and the openness. If there was coercion or deception, I never noticed it. I went along with what the men wanted sexually because of my burning need to be accepted.

In puberty, things got worse. I often asked myself, 'Why am I different? Am I a freak, a Queen, a transsexual, a transvestite, a pansy, a fruit?'

At any stage through this difficult developmental process, any male adult who takes a boy seriously and provides empathy is likely to be viewed as a god-like figure. The attachment is much stronger if, as in my case, the boy is being emotionally neglected or physically and psychologically abused at home.

Things go wrong for boys when they no longer want to participate in sex and complain or refuse to carry out the adults' wishes. Some men's sexual demands are painful and thoroughly obnoxious. Paedophiles and pederasts are usually stimulated by the chase and the grooming process and they put a great deal of effort into the seduction process. When they sense that children are in their power, their sexual priority becomes more obvious and the friendship aspect declines. Bright children spot that 'he's only nice when he wants sex' and they try to restore the emotional aspects of the relationship. They are then rejected and, hurt, they withdraw.

The paedophile rejects in a very cruel way, subjecting the discarded victim to as many emotional 'put downs' as are necessary to get rid of him. I became trapped in this scenario again and again. When I tried to opt out of unacceptable sexual practices, the men routinely told me that, 'It's your fault. You came here voluntarily. You knew what you were getting into. I didn't make you come. And you've done it before. You wanted it. You are responsible. It's no good complaining. How dare you lead me on and then say "No".'

I found these confrontations very distressing. I believed and trusted the men and I was cast aside again and again. I thought that the rejection was 'my fault' and did not realise that I was being used. I believed that the men cared about me (as they had purported to do) and when things went wrong, it must be my fault.

This is one of the insidious aspects of child sexual abuse by paedophiles and pederasts. They are highly skilled manipulators. One moment, everything is wonderful and the child feels good about himself and, in a flash, everything changes and the child is left carrying the guilt and responsibility for something that, because of his needs, his level of development and lack of information, is not his fault.

Whenever this happened to me, I systematically went searching for a replacement father figure who would provide that attention and affection that I yearned for. The seduction/grooming/use and discard procedures were repeated by numerous men . . . far too many to count. When the affection stopped and I realised that the man in question only wanted me for sex, I felt dirty and wanted the relationship to change. Each time, I desperately tried to restore the friendship that was so enjoyable to me but the adult made it clear that I was only a sex object. I then had to opt out and start looking for another paedophile.

Boys who believe that they are homosexual are at very high risk of sexual abuse because they are invariably lonely, confused, sad and easily identified by adult predators. They suffer taunts and bullying from peers and sometimes from their well-meaning, macho fathers. Their parents try to over-protect them, hoping that it's only a 'passing phase' and the problem will go away. Teachers and parents pick on them to try to toughen them up.

Girls get along well with them but they suffer ridicule from other boys if they befriend them. Group cohesion requires that they join in the verbal abuse. When they encounter an understanding male adult, homosexual boys are overwhelmed with relief and gratitude and sexual behaviour almost appears as a natural part of the relationship.

Because of their conditioning, boys are unable to report sexual abuse. They believe either that they are to blame or that it did no harm or that it happened because they were homosexual or perceived as different (rather than that they were young, needed affection and happened to be in the wrong place at the wrong time). Boys seldom identify sexual abuse for what it is because they like some of the sexual touching or they liked the perpetrator and see only the kindness. Young male victims are terrified of revealing that they may be homosexual because, even if they have had no previous contact with police, they know that society is homophobic. Those who try to report abuse are often disbelieved or their mothers 'go off at the deep end', inflicting further psychological abuse on the victims.

It is very easy for child molesters to select boys who have already been subjected to early sexualisation. The vast majority of child molesters were victims themselves; a victim recognises another's sense of isolation, sadness and low self-esteem. He recognises the signs of premature sexual experience.

I became a juvenile child molester at the age of seven when I had sexual intercourse with a younger girl. At age nine, I had intercourse with my young male cousin. There was nothing unusual about that. Firstly, it had been happening to me throughout my life. Secondly, my social group consisted of sexually experienced boys, many of whom were already having sexual intercourse with their younger brothers. One of the paedophiles was using his three-year-old sister.

Paradoxically, the only occasion when I was 'caught' was when I had done nothing. My mates were having sex with the little girl next door. I stood and watched but did not intervene even though I knew that sex with girls was wrong. The others wanted me to join in and I refused. The child's mother sensed that there was something amiss and came looking for her. Because I was in the group, I was held equally to blame and received another thrashing from my father.

My parents were horrified that their son was involved in sex with girls at such an early age. They curbed my freedom entirely and appointed my brother John to supervise my every movement. The irony was that he was the most frequent and persistent predator.

111

My childhood, for what it was worth, ended at the age of ten when I was sent to work at the stables before and after school. I fed the horses twice a day, seven days of the week and it was my job to clean them out. When they were ready for racing, I was given the awesome task of keeping watch over them to make sure that no-one crept into the stables to drug them. This was lonely and frightening because, in stables, there are always strange noises and rustlings. Armed with nothing more than a torch, it was difficult to know whether the sounds came from mice in the loft, restless animals or dangerous men bent on 'nobbling' the horses about to race. I took my role seriously and was very conscious of the fact that I had the care of thousands of pounds worth of horseflesh which, overnight, could make us very rich or very poor.

I was often given responsibility for exercising the horses . . . sometimes two at a time. This involved starting work at four o'clock in the morning, sometimes working a fourteen-hour day. I had to work on race days and at weekends to let paid staff take time off. There was no increase in my spending money and if I needed payment in advance, my mother charged interest at the current bank rate. I felt like a little old slave; I ate, I slept and I worked. Dad often made me take the day off school to help him out. I was a bright kid but I had little success in the classroom.

In the end, life wasn't worth living except for the fact that I loved the horses and, by gentleness, could get them to do things that my father failed to achieve by bullying. When I protested that I was being unfairly treated, I was told, 'Go! Get out! You won't survive for a week without me. You'll never manage on your own.'

My mother vacillated between supporting my father and persuading me that she and the family business could not manage without my labour. I felt trapped and began to think about suicide.

When I was eleven, Ray, an apprentice jockey, came to live with us. Ray was an instant success in the saddle and soon began to win races, earning thousands and thousands of pounds. Ray became my father's golden-haired wonder boy and he, in turn, enjoyed dad's approval. My father suddenly changed his lifestyle, spending more time at the stables and less time at the pub.

Ray soon realised that I was the family scapegoat and he joined in the fun. While I remained responsible for much of the manual work and acted as 'strapper', my efforts were derided and even sabotaged. Ray enjoyed getting me into trouble, blaming me for anything that went wrong. I hated him and was jealous.

Dad was never satisfied with my efforts and enjoyed humiliating me, especially in the presence of clients. He taunted me with my uselessness: 'He'll never be good for anything . . . He'll never hold a job down for more than five minutes.' He implied that I was fortunate because no-one else would tolerate my uselessness as he did; no other employer would want me. If I became defensive, he retaliated with threats of violence: 'You have no rights around here, I own you. You're mine and I can do what I like with you.'

When I was twelve, dad decided that I needed toughening up so he put me on the same harsh exercise and discipline regime as the jockeys.

On race days, I had the responsibility of walking the horses, one in each hand, along the busy highway to Flemington Race Course. There, my job was to stand at the front of the stall to protect the horses from being drugged by crooks. If there was a horse racing at the end of the day, I would not be allowed to leave my post until after the last race. Dad was occupied with his friends and it never occurred to him to give me a break or bring me a snack and a drink.

I longed for dad's approval . . . a pat on the back, an arm across the shoulder . . . a word of recognition acknowledging that, for a twelve year old, I was doing a relatively good job. He praised Ray endlessly and seemed to take a fiendish delight in the knowledge that he was hurting me. I put on a brave face, went back home, fed the horses and pretended that it didn't matter. But, of course, it mattered a lot.

To cope with constant rejection, I had to become proficient in hiding my feelings from other family members. My father became angry when he found that he could no longer provoke me. I escaped more and more to my bedroom and appeared only for meals. The bedroom was both a prison and a safe haven.

At fourteen, I left school and took an apprenticeship as a welder. I wasn't interested in welding but my father thought that it was a masculine job and it would 'make a man' of me. I wanted to be a Methodist minister or a salesman. My father was furious. He said that no son of his was going to have a poofter job. Why did I want to do women's work anyway? I needed a real man's job.

I started my apprenticeship with considerable resentment. A contributing factor was that my parents kept most of my wages for themselves. Although I was working an eight-hour day with an eight o'clock start and attended evening classes, my father insisted that I cleaned out the stables before dawn and fed the horses both before and after work.

113

I completed the apprenticeship and, with great apprehension, I announced that I had accepted a job as a pastry chef. My father was furious. He said that he wouldn't let me work alongside a bunch of 'poofters'. This was the last straw and I told him that his mates (whom I named) were the ones who best matched his definition of 'poofter'. He flew into a rage but never invited me to explain what I meant by this remark.

At about this time, I decided, subconsciously if not consciously, that the only way to gain control of my own life was to increase my weight. I was tired of being pushed around and I suddenly realised that fat people could not be pushed. I began to eat . . . and eat . . . and eat. I increased my weight but failed to protect myself from my father and brothers.

I did not view sexual interest in children as being wrong until I reached my late teens. This is understandable given that my age had not been a deterrent to my own abusers and my school peer group consisted of sexually experienced children of all ages. Furthermore, until now, I had always been more interested in older men than young children.

I was about twenty when I first became really aware that the tables had turned and I now found young boys sexually attractive. I was visiting a farm with friends when a child came into the room. He sat on the carpet playing with a model sports car and, every now and again, he looked towards me and smiled. Eventually, he came to sit by me and showed me the vehicle. I admired it and pointed out some of the significant details.

He put the car down and put his hand on my sock. He then walked his fingers up my leg. I expected him to stop at my knee but he didn't . . . he continued and fingered his way up my thigh. I interpreted his action as sexual teasing. I assumed that the child was sexually aware and knew what he was doing. I experienced arousal and, feeling very embarrassed, I moved his hand away. He merely saw this as fun and started the whole procedure again. As we were in adult company, I made an excuse to go to the bathroom. With the door locked, I looked in the mirror and took stock of myself. I recognised that I was sexually excited and conveniently forgot that what I wanted was wrong. I rationalised that the little boy was a mirror image of myself as a child but I didn't say, 'No . . . it's wrong'. I did quite the opposite and argued that the boy was 'most probably homosexual' and 'it's probably happened before'. I told myself that he needed affection and attention just as I had needed it and I could find more reasons for encouraging than discouraging his attention. In the end, I withdrew, not so much because I saw it as wrong but because the child was 'too young . . . too little'.

On another occasion, I recognised the sexual 'come ons' of a nine-year-old boy, Mike, who visited our house with his sixteen-year-old brother. Mike introduced sexual innuendos and 'dirty talk' and I was not at all surprised when he told me that he had been used for anal sex by his brother.

It would have been the easiest thing in the world to have developed a sexual relationship with the lad because he was clearly looking for a male adult to give him attention. I recognised what was happening and pulled myself back. I went looking for the sixteen-year-old brother instead.

A few weeks ago, I attended a barbecue at the home of married friends who had three young sons, aged eight, ten and twelve. I enjoyed the boys' company and they enjoyed mine to the extent that they invited me to leave the adults and accompany them to the park. The parents gave their approval and away we went. The boys were laughing and teasing me and each other. They climbed trees, performed somersaults and did acrobatics on their bikes using only the rear wheels. And all of the time, their faces were radiant and they called, 'Watch me . . . Look at this . . . Have you seen anyone do this before?' They threw their arms around me spontaneously, jumped on me and tickled me. I was attracted by their innocence, their vitality and trust and I was sexually aroused by the ten year old. He used sexual innuendos, put his arms round my waist and patted my buttocks. I thought, 'He's been abused. He's done this before. He wants sex.'

Fortunately, I recognised what was happening and stepped back. This was very hard to do because, when you have been accustomed to sex equating with comfort and attention, it is very difficult to remove yourself from an enjoyable, intimate 'buddy' situation and return to the role of the responsible adult. It is even more difficult if, as in this case, the children are enjoying themselves and plead with you not to stop.

I don't mind admitting that I have, on many occasions, been only a hair's breadth from committing offences with young boys. Child abuse has a dehumanising effect on victims and I often find that I have no conscience when other people would expect me to have one. And although I am now in my late forties, I am still obsessed with sex.

I think that it also needs to be made clear that someone with my history has no conscience about sex per se. I do not withdraw from sexual situations with children because it is wrong and against the law. I make no pretence that I back off because I 'don't want to damage another child in the same way that I was damaged'. Looking back on my life, it was the betrayal of trust, the psychological abuse and the rejection that hurt the most. The sex came with the package. As a consequence, I find myself rejecting sexual situations only for pragmatic reasons. I am not inhibited by conscience, morality or fear of the justice system. After all, the justice system did nothing to protect me and I learned nothing about conscience from the models in my home environment. And it is so easy to transfer blame to children because large numbers of boys are so obviously sexually curious. Large numbers are obviously sexually experienced and are looking for affection from male adults. Paedophiles and pederasts are social misfits who are also looking for affection and approval. Some boys pretend to be more sophisticated than they really are. Those who have been abused by their older brothers may feel a sense of achievement in the seduction of an adult. For the sexually sophisticated boy, another abuser is 'no big deal . . . after all I've done it before and the others didn't give me what this man is offering'.

One of the dangers is, of course, that offenders looking for victims are likely to put sinister connotations on spontaneous and innocent affection, touching and normal sexual curiosity from a child whom they find attractive.

Men who are sexually attracted to children are surrounded by temptations and opportunities for abuse. They attract boys who are readily available for sex and they attract those seeking the affection and approval that is missing at home.

To stop abuse from occurring, there has to be early identification of the risk. I have to spot seductive children before sexual arousal occurs so that I withdraw from situations which might increase temptation. I have to identify the signs of sexual interest at the very early stages and get away. Once arousal has occurred, it becomes much more difficult to step back from the situation.

An adult who is a survivor of sexual abuse recognises the sexually and emotionally damaged child and forms a bond, consciously or unconsciously. An adult who has been a victim and assumes that a child is interested in sex may justify sexual contact by telling himself that he will make sex a better experience for that child than the child has had at the hands of other men. Paradoxically, he then goes on to use the same behaviours and the same methods of silencing and discarding the child that he experienced in childhood.

When I was twenty-five, I fell in love with a girl who was later to become my wife. We had a stunning sexual relationship. She was a superb chef and, together, we opened a restaurant. We worked hard and built up a very successful business. On our wedding day, my mother pronounced, 'You're married! Thank God for that! We were afraid that you were going to turn out to be one of those poofters.'

Unfortunately, without realising what I had done, I had married someone who was a mirror image of my father and mother (combined). She was competitive and materialistic, demanding all of my energy, my devotion, my commitment, my time, giving nothing but sexual, verbal and emotional abuse in return. She withheld sex on our wedding day and most days thereafter and it took me many years to understand what was happening. By that time, we had three children whom I loved dearly.

At the age of eight, I had made a conscious decision that, if I ever had children, I would be a different kind of parent to my own and, fortunately, I was able to make most of the necessary changes. I used my parents as models to avoid and I set out to be a better listener, a better communicator, a more respectful parent than I had ever known. These efforts were rewarded when, after twenty years, I left the marriage and my teenage children elected to live with me.

I took a long hard look at myself and I was shocked by what I saw. I suffered (and still suffer) from low self-esteem and view everything that I've done in life in negative terms. I constantly put myself down and even when there is evidence of my success, I view it as a fluke or worse, undeserved. I am still useless Jim, ugly Jim, Jim who could never please and never did anything right.

As an adult, I still longed to be accepted by my parents and brothers but I remained the scapegoat and misfit. The more they rejected me, the more I tried to please them. They seemed to take an insidious delight in putting me down.

Even after my marriage and their own, my brothers continued to wield power over me. They were difficult to resist because, at times, they could be sensitive, supportive and generous and helped me financially when I was buying the business and needed a home after separating from my wife. I wanted to resist because they were also bullies who belittled me because I failed to meet their stereotyped macho expectations. They taunted me constantly with sexual enticement and I capitulated to my half-brother when I was thirty.

My second brother, John, used me for sex until I was forty six. I remember the last occasion very well. He was going to check up on a property for friends who were on an overseas holiday and he asked me to go with him. We went from room to room and eventually reached a luxurious bedroom with a king-sized waterbed. My brother suggested that we should try out the bed and, of course, we did. He used me for anal sex. I felt degraded, disgusted, dirty and incredibly weak but there was also a strange sense of relief. I suddenly realised that I no longer felt indebted to my brother. At long last, he had managed to do what he had paid for forty years earlier and, with that, he had lost his hold over me.

All three of us were 'screwed up' psychologically and made a mess of our lives. We drifted from relationship to relationship and job to job. My macho brothers are both bi-sexual but lack the guts to admit it, even to themselves. I am convinced that they were both abused by my father but I have never had the courage to ask them. I am equally certain that they abused their own children who are now abusing their children.

Two years ago, after considerable professional counselling, I 'came out' as a gay person and joined the gay community. I decided to call a family meeting to announce my decision. I shall remember that meeting for as long as I live. I had prepared and rehearsed my speech and joined the group apprehensively. Five of my abusers were present. When I informed the gathering that I now wished to be regarded as a gay man, jaws dropped and there was a gasp of incredulity. My father was the first to recover his composure with the pompous announcement that he no longer regarded me as his son and he did not wish to see or speak to me ever again.

'How can I face my friends and admit to fathering a son who has sex with other men? I'd be a laughing stock,' he said. 'My God! You might have AIDS!'

My brothers took the lead from my father and told me that I'd disgraced the family name. They announced, almost in unison, that they, too, would have to disown me because they could not cope with the shame of having a poofter brother . . . It would be embarrassing to have me visit their homes.

They all turned away in disdain . . . yes, the man who had used me for sex when I was only a baby and the man who had raped me and molested me throughout my childhood . . . the men who had raped me in my primary school years and the man who used his power over me throughout my life and had used me for sex only a few weeks before the meeting. They all suddenly rejected me and told me that I should be ashamed of myself!

I looked at the brother who had controlled and terrified me for forty long years and I suddenly saw him for what he was . . . a balding, insensitive, fifty-six-year-old bigot who had no comprehension of the damage that he had caused.

I looked at my half-brother, now in his sixties and saw a very confused and unhappy man. I looked at the family photographs on the sideboard and felt nothing but sadness. There was the picture of me as a baby, surrounded by smiling parents and brothers. I looked at the date on the back and realised that my father had already sexually abused me when that photograph was taken. I longed to ask, 'Why? How dare you do that to such a tiny child? What possible satisfaction could you have gained from harming a baby? Have you no idea of the damage that you caused? Don't you realise what you did to me?'

On that day, two years ago, my relatives lost the capacity to hurt me because I no longer wanted or needed their love and approval. I turned away and left the house for the last time with a great sense of relief. I was free of them . . . but I can never be free of my past.

6

'It did me no harm—I did no harm'

My childhood was somewhat different to that experienced by other contributors to this book.

My name is James and I am the younger of two sons of two caring parents living in a stable and relatively happy home environment. We were an unremarkable family except for the fact that my parents belonged to a nudist club and I was not subjected to the customary taboos about the human body.

To the best of my knowledge, there were no major upsets in my childhood. I was deprived of nothing that I needed and despite the disgrace I brought to my family, my parents have continued to support me. This must be especially difficult for Dad, given that his professional life involves the justice system and he now has a twenty-one-year-old son in jail with a ten-year sentence for sexually abusing children.

My obsession with sex began when I was eight years old. Unlike most of my prison colleagues my early sexualisation was not at the hands of an adult but at the instigation of another eight year old, albeit one who had been abused by adults and was already very experienced in sexual matters.

Most people imagine that peer group curiosity is normal and harmless. I certainly saw nothing wrong with it when my new friend Rick initiated the game of 'You show me yours and I'll show you mine'. When Rick suggested that we might go beyond looking and tickling and extend to mutual masturbation, that also felt good; in fact it felt so good that we did it almost every day.

One day, Rick asked if he could put his penis inside my mouth.

That seemed a stupid thing to do and I refused. He didn't insist. Instead, he knelt down on the ground and put my penis in his mouth. At first I thought that he must be crazy but when it began to feel tickley, I liked it. And when Rick asked me to suck him I could scarcely refuse.

This was repeated almost daily until Rick got bored and asked for something different. His next suggestion was for me to stick my penis inside his bottom. I laughed . . . it sounded absurd. Bottoms were for other things. Rick noted my hesitation and assured me that he would do the same and make it feel good for me. He convinced me that I would like it so I agreed. Rick took off his pants and bent over. I did as he told me. I was amazed by his behaviour but when he said, 'Now, it's my turn', I didn't object. Thereafter this became a habit.

We had a cubby house in the bush near where I lived. We met there daily. It never occurred to me that what we were doing was wrong.

About four months later, Rick and I went for a bike ride on a track by the river. There, we met a man who was fishing. His name was Ron. He was about forty years old. Rick greeted Ron like an old friend and it was obvious that they knew each other quite well. Rick propped his bike against a tree and he went with Ron into the van which was parked on the track. He then beckoned me to follow.

Rick immediately dropped his pants. He must have spotted the look of surprise on my face because he said, 'It's OK. Ron knows what we do. I've done it before.'

I felt scared but Ron reassured me, 'Look, it's alright—I'm taking mine off', and he removed his pants. I didn't want to be the odd one out so I dropped mine and agreed to join in the game. At first, we fondled each other. Then, Ron asked if he could suck Rick. He agreed and I watched. Then, it was my turn. Ron then wanted us to reciprocate. I wasn't very happy about this but, as he'd done it to me I couldn't really refuse. I hated it. I felt as if I was about to choke. The taste was awful. This was vastly different to the games I'd played with Rick. I protested that Ron tasted yuck. He resolved this by giving me lollies. He then asked me to put my penis inside Rick. I tried while Ron watched and played with himself. When I got fed up, he instructed Rick to do the same thing to me. Then he said, 'It's my turn now'. He tried but failed. I cried out with pain and was relieved when he stopped. He tried to do it with Rick too but eventually he accepted defeat. Then, out of the blue, Rick asked

Ron to show me how he could 'make white stuff'. I sat and watched in amazement. Then we left and I cycled home.

Rick and I often met Ron in his van after that and the routine was always the same: he did things that were pleasurable to us and then said, 'Now, it's my turn'.

Ron then started bringing his friend Jim to join in the fun. It was clear to me that Rick had previously been sexually involved with both men. My relationship with Rick continued for all of four years, from the age of eight to the age of twelve. During that time, I became obsessed with sex and sought sexual activity of any kind at every conceivable opportunity. This obsession has remained with me throughout my life. Looking back, I realise that I knew very little about the two men. I believe that one was married but I have no idea what either of them did for a living or whether they had children. We had only one reason for meeting.

At age thirteen, I developed a relationship with a girl of the same age. She was sexually experienced and agreed to intercourse. This sexual relationship lasted a year; I enjoyed it but I realised that I still had strong urges to have sex with boys instead of girls.

In early adolescence, it became harder to persuade other boys of my own age to participate in any form of homosexual activity. They were now only interested in girls and I had to turn to younger boys. It was much easier to persuade them to join in, either because they had been taught to obey adults (and, to young children, I was 'grown-up') or because they were more curious than my peers or because they were already sexually experienced. I was attracted to boys of four years upwards and found that I could easily engage them in sexual activity, using little persuasion and no force. No bribes were necessary. The routine was always the same: I introduced conversation about sex, touched their genitals, enquired whether they liked it and, when their interest was assured, invited them to reciprocate. Few had the confidence to refuse when I announced, 'Now, it's my turn'.

When I was fourteen, another man came into my life. Jack was in his forties, lived alone and worked as an attendant at the local swimming pool. He had lived in Holland during the second world war and captivated me with stories of the German occupation and his own exploits. He got on well with the local children who spent their days at the pool during their summer holidays. Jack played in the pool with them and carried them on his shoulders. He threw them into the water, chased them and tickled them. I was a keen swimmer and went to the pool regularly. One day, the pool was empty. Jack was alone and he invited me into his office. He enquired whether I liked girls—whether I'd ever had a girlfriend. I said 'Yes'. He wanted to know what I'd done with girls. He then took some pornographic magazines out of his drawer and showed me photographs of men and women engaged in sexual intercourse. This was my introduction to pornography and I was curious, fascinated and stimulated by what I saw.

Jack took advantage of my interest. He enquired whether I had ever had sex. I told him about the girls but kept quiet about the boys. He undid my shorts. I didn't stop him when he fondled me.

Whenever I went to the pool thereafter, I went into Jack's office and we played around with each other. Obviously, it was unsafe doing this in a public place and although the danger added to the excitement, Jack realised that he was at risk of being caught. He invited me to his house, using the excuse that he wanted to show me some porn magazines and videos. I knew, of course, that there would be more involved than watching television and I accepted the invitation. As it was the school holidays and my parents were back at work, I managed to spend the day with Jack without explaining my whereabouts to my family.

Jack invited me into a spare room which was furnished as a bed-sitting room, equipped with television and video. He brought some magazines and videos and asked whether I would like to see them. He then showed a porn movie involving lesbians. This was mind-boggling for a fourteen year old and, of course, it provided the necessary stimulation.

I visited Jack quite regularly over the following two years. He took other boys to the house and told me of his exploits with them. I was never jealous of Jack's interest in other boys. Our sole purpose for meeting was to view pornography and experience personal sexual gratification. There was no pretence of liking or caring for each other.

The kids in the neighbourhood learned of my visits and, knowing that Jack was 'weird', they ostracised me.

From the age of fourteen to sixteen, I worked as a volunteer for a historical society. There, I met Paul, a thirty-one-year-old professional who was accompanied by his young cousin, James, aged twelve. I was immediately attracted to the boy. He was cute, and I had an overwhelming urge to have sex with him.

When I eventually managed to separate James from his cousin, I steered the conversation to girls, then sex. This proved unfruitful because James' sexual experience was limited to a glimpse of a magazine which contained pictures of nude women. I tried all my usual tricks to stimulate his interest but none of them worked. When I ran out of ideas, I did a quick memory scan of the repertoire of methods used by men on me and, in desperation, I asked the boy whether he had been circumcised. As it happened, James was circumcised, knew more about the subject than I did and wasn't remotely interested in talking about it. By this time, the desire to seduce him was quite desperate. I asked if he was interested in learning about sex and, to my surprise and irritation, he gave a very firm 'No'. Met with such firmness, I did not persist.

A week later, Paul came to the museum without James. I was disappointed and asked where the boy was. Paul said that James lived in Queensland and had only been staying with him for the school vacation. He then enquired whether I had any time to spare. I said that I had. He invited me to have lunch at his flat and explained that he had photographs which would be of interest to me.

Paul made pancakes for lunch, after which he showed me photos of historical buildings and military equipment. When I had seen them all, he handed me another photograph album. I sensed instantly that there was something different about this book and when I turned the pages, I saw photographs of nude boys. I was surprised to say the least.

'James told me about your invitation,' Paul said.

'Which invitation?'

'Your invitation to teach him about sex.'

I blushed with embarrassment. I feared that Paul was going to punish me but he didn't. He stroked my thighs over my jeans until I was sexually aroused. We talked sex non-stop for a couple of hours. Paul had travelled around the world to Asia, Africa and Europe. He told me about the different kinds of sex he'd had with boys in countries overseas and showed me the photographs that he'd taken. It was quite clear that, although some of them were several years old, the reminiscences still excited him. We repeated the activities several times before that afternoon was over and I agreed to meet Paul again. I saw him several times but he knew that it was James that I really wanted.

At the age of sixteen I was reported for sexual misconduct with a young boy.

My behaviour was assumed to be the normal sexual curiosity of a normal adolescent and no-one took it seriously. This was the only occasion on which a child reported me.

At the age of seventeen, I left home to join the defence forces. For a time, I was happy with my lot. There were lots of challenges and life was interesting. Then, the urges returned. I tried to fight them by joining clubs and having sex with women and prostitutes but this failed to provide satisfaction.

I went to local swimming pools and started 'perving' on young boys using the toilets and changing rooms. I bought nudist magazines and used them for stimulation. Interestingly, after spending years at nudist clubs with my parents and finding the nude body singularly uninteresting, I suddenly found male nudism tantalising. A photograph of a twelve year old became the subject of my sexual fantasies.

I placed myself in greater danger by becoming involved in clubs for children, teaching them bush walking, mapping skills and fitness. I enjoy being with kids and am much more comfortable with them than with adults. Children are accepting, pliable, affectionate, responsive, trusting and sincere. When I joined, I didn't deliberately set out to seduce them but of course, that's what happened. I was content with the company of some boys when I did not find them sexually appealing. I was drawn to others spontaneously without understanding the reason for the attraction.

In a sports group, I met a boy named Mark, aged thirteen. The other boys said that he was unpopular and untrustworthy. I knew that I was taking a risk but I befriended him. We got along extremely well. He talked to me about his family, his friends, his school life, his hobbies and sporting interests and I listened attentively. I became his special friend. He introduced me to his parents and eventually they invited me for dinner. As they learned to trust me, I was invited to special weekends with them and, inevitably, I offered to take him out on excursions to give Mark's parents a break.

Mark confided in me that he was in love with a girl called Ann. He had no previous experience with girls and sought my advice on how to develop a sexual relationship. This gave me the opportunity that I needed and I offered to help him to develop sex techniques. I arranged to meet Mark the following weekend and obtained his parents' permission to take him fishing. I looked forward to this meeting.

As we sat on the river bank, I tentatively enquired whether he had given any more thought to his plan to seduce Ann. He had not. I asked him to pretend that I was his girlfriend and do to me what he planned to do to her. He looked at me in astonishment and burst out laughing. That attempt failed abysmally.

Eventually, I tricked him into dropping his tracksuit pants . . . then his underpants and I fondled him.

When I took him home, he surprised me by asking his parents if he could stay at my flat overnight so that we could have an early start for the fishing trip the following day. His parents enquired whether this would be convenient to me, and, of course, I assured them that I was very happy to care for their son.

When we arrived at my flat, I prepared the fish for cooking. Mark was in the lounge. He was quiet and I peeped around the door to see what he was doing. His face was hidden behind a copy of Penthouse. I crept up behind him and slipped my hand down the front of his pants. He was already aroused from reading the magazines and he did not resist my touching.

After a shower and our evening meal, I put on a porn video. Mark didn't object. I enquired whether he was still interested in hearing about sex and he confirmed that he was. He was very reluctant to participate but persuasion proved effective. I tried to reproduce what we had seen but he soon lost interest.

Mark and I occupied a double bed. The following morning it was raining heavily and we had to cancel the fishing trip. While I washed the dishes, Mark watched a video which showed sex in a shower scene. I said that I was about to have a shower and invited him to join me. We spent most of that day engaged in sexual activity.

Some weeks later Mark confided that he had been successful in seducing Ann but we continued to meet and Mark never told our special secret.

During this period, Trent, aged twelve, introduced himself to me at the swimming pool. He was a friend of Mark and knew of our fishing expeditions. We swam together for a while and then sat on the grass to rest. Trent enquired whether I could take him fishing. I agreed and we arranged to meet at the swimming pool the next day. Before we went our separate ways Trent opened his school bag, pulled out a copy of Playboy and asked me if I would keep it for him because he didn't want his parents to know that he read rude magazines. He flipped through the pages and showed me a picture of a girl that he 'fancied'. I tentatively enquired whether he'd like to have sex with her. He said 'Yes'. This gave me the opportunity to enquire whether he knew what sex was. He replied, 'It's when you put your thing inside a girl'.

I informed him that there was much more to sex than that, and, if he was interested, I would be willing to give him lessons in sex education. He responded with a firm 'No' and left.

A few days later, I answered a knock at the door. It was Trent. He said that he'd come to collect his magazine. He sat in the lounge and thumbed through it, then enquired whether I had others. Trent responded sexually to the visual stimulation and I took advantage of this.

Trent had no previous sexual experience but he was curious and responsive to my suggestions. He asked me to keep this from Mark because his friend would not like him if he knew that he was having sex with a man. Trent was unaware that his mate Mark had already been in my bed. I was feeling very pleased with myself because I now had not one but two sexual partners who were also best friends. I fantasised about sex with both boys in a threesome but when I suggested this to Trent, he rejected it outright, and I respected his wishes.

In the meantime, my reputation for being 'good with kids' spread across the base and I was often asked to babysit for married couples with young families and their friends.

On one such occasion, I was invited to mind Joshua aged seven and his five-year-old sister, Tina. Before they went to bed, we played at chasing and tickling games during which time I touched Joshua's penis and pretended that it was an accident. I watched to see if there was any reaction and there was none.

I put Tina to bed and tucked her in. Then, I went to Joshua's room and offered to read him a story. He chose the story and I sat on the bed, holding the book with one hand, putting the other around the child. I put my hand under the sheet and stroked him on top of his pyjamas. He raised no objection. When I reached his groin he said, 'Ooh, that tickles'.

I asked whether he liked what I was doing but he merely shrugged his shoulders and said, 'It tickles'.

I invited Joshua to tickle me. He did and thought that was fun. I then put his hand on my penis and suggested that we should play at, 'You show me yours and I'll show you mine'.

I persisted in trying to develop his interest in sex and offered to demonstrate how grown-ups make white stuff. We went to the bathroom together. Joshua was not at all impressed by my efforts, and said, 'It only looks like glue'. He went to bed and I kissed him goodnight. I slept in the spare room. The following morning, Joshua woke up at dawn and came into my bed. His parents and sister were still asleep. I introduced sexual touching again and Joshua giggled under the sheets.

I was often asked to babysit for Joshua and his sister and many of these occasions provided opportunities for sexual contact.

There have been many other boys in my life . . . probably forty or fifty boys and maybe twenty girls. The pattern of seduction has been repeated again and again. I took boys fishing, I met them at swimming pools, I introduced sex talk and few resisted genital touching and oral sex. The resistance only came when they were asked to reciprocate. Because of their high level of sexual arousal, boys are easily seduced. They are excited when they talk about sex . . . not the sex of the birds and the bees and reproduction, but the kind of sex that would horrify their parents. They want to know more about their own bodies.

Over the years, I remembered the impact of Paul's photographs of his child sexual partners in Africa and Asia. Eventually, I bought a camera and started taking photographs of children's genitals. I used these records to stimulate sexual arousal when I was alone and they provided reminders of the attractiveness of children's bodies. This step eventually led to my downfall when a photograph fell into the hands of police. I was charged with twelve offences, pleaded guilty and received a ten-year sentence. I was absolutely shocked . . . totally unprepared for this because, although I knew, at an intellectual level, that I was breaking the law, I believed that the law was wrong and I was doing no harm. I rationalised that the men who introduced me to sex did me no harm: I was a willing participant. And, after all, I always asked children whether they liked what I was doing. Few said 'No'. If they did, I might try to persuade them to change their minds but I never used force; force was never necessary. Many of the boys were actively looking for sex . . . especially those of around twelve or thirteen upwards. They knew about my reputation (from other boys) and they came with the intention of joining in the fun. How could that be wrong? How could I have a conscience about my activities with them? Even with the youngest children, I gave them a choice . . . didn't I? If they said 'No' (and few did), I merely returned to the activity that we engaged in prior to the rejection and tried again later. If a child persisted in saying 'No', I settled for whatever he or she was prepared to give. With practice, you get a strong sense of which children will be willing participants but there's always an element of challenge and 'trial and error' involved.

In general, I found that more children were triggered by sexual curiosity than by the need for affection. Few were sexually experienced prior to their first contact with me. I selected children who were physically attractive. Boys were especially appealing in their eagerness to learn about sex and although I know that it isn't my place to teach them, I am sure that they were pleased to find an adult who would let them talk about their sexual urges and feelings.

I always felt that the law was out of touch with reality. I argue that kids need sex with experienced partners and the age of consent should be removed or at least lowered to, say, age twelve or thirteen for both boys and girls. After all, if it was so bad for them, wouldn't more than one of the seventy or so children have complained about me? Some came back repeatedly over prolonged periods of time. If I was as wicked as the justice system implied, wouldn't more children have rejected me? And if I'm at fault, surely society has to take equal responsibility? From infancy, children are exposed to sex on television, on the covers of magazines and even posters outside newsagencies. Parents watch porn movies and justify their behaviour on the basis that their children are 'too young to understand'. Children hear sexual conversations and innuendos in their homes and peer groups. And yet adult society consistently and persistently denies that children are sexual beings . . . that boys have strong sexual urges and sexual interests from a very early age. Even my own liberal-minded parents, who asked lots of detailed questions when they learned of my arrest, avoided questions about my sexual preferences. My problem was a taboo subject and not even they could refer to it.

Adults weave romantic notions about children's innocence, conveniently forgetting their own curiosity and sexual excitement in childhood. It suits parents' own needs to imagine that children are deaf, blind and totally insensitive to the highly sexual environments in which they live.

Adult society refuses to recognise the fact that children do not necessarily view genital touching as bad, unpleasant or unsafe . . . and some children enjoy it. Until that simple fact is recognised and incorporated in child protection programmes, children will remain vulnerable to people like me.

7

Child prostitution and the law

I am twenty-two years old and am currently serving a ten-year jail sentence for sexual offences against a boy. I would like to be in a position to tell you the whole of my story, openly and honestly, but I fear that to do so would put my life at risk. Even though I am assured of anonymity, I can trust no-one.

The reason for my fear is that my introduction to sexual abuse was at the age of nine at the hands of a police officer. Not only did he use me for sex, he was also the organiser of a paedophile ring and the operator of a brothel for men who wanted sex with young boys. This was no ordinary brothel: the regular clients were doctors, clergymen, a Lord Mayor, an alderman, well-known media personalities and prominent businessmen. Some held the most powerful positions in the State . . . magistrates, a judge, lawyers, a State politician, the very men who are responsible for upholding law and order.

Although I am in prison, I cannot escape from my abusers. I see their faces in newspapers and on television. When new prisoners talk about their cases, I sometimes recognise the name of the lawyer or the police officer who prosecuted them and the judge who sentenced them. The hypocrisy sickens me.

I listen to those prisoners' stories in silence because I know that if I revealed the details of my past, I would soon experience a fatal 'accident'; the men who controlled me as a prostitute would have no qualms about arranging my death to protect themselves. Having a loaded gun stuck in your mouth when you are a child creates a lasting impression.

I was the third of six children in a working-class family living in the inner suburbs of Sydney. My father was a truck driver and my mother sold cosmetics for one of those American companies that demand total commitment to their products. Their sales strategies were clearly successful because we saw little of my mother during our childhood years. Dad was out driving, mum was out selling and we children were left to our own devices. When Dad was at home, he was unhappy about Mum being out. It wasn't long before he was spending his spare time with his mates at the pub. When he came home, Dad was often drunk and cranky and he took out his frustration on the kids. The following day, he couldn't remember what he had done. Through this trick of amnesia he was able to discount our bruises and black eyes with a quick apology and a promise not to do it again.

We moved house and changed schools many times in those early years and the sense of isolation was intensified by the instability of our living conditions. Although I had an older brother and sister, I was a lonely child. There was a substantial gap between our ages and I never felt that I knew anyone or that anyone knew or cared for me. My mother provided sales demonstrations on most evenings and, when she became a regional manager, she often went to meetings during the day. She either left us alone in the house or in the care of our older sister who was neither old enough nor sufficiently knowledgeable to take responsibility for our well-being and safety. I can truthfully say that my sister brought me up. As she became an adolescent, she bitterly resented the imposition placed upon her. Her friends were able to go out with boys to discos and clubs while she was expected to stay at home, provide meals, bath us and put us to bed. She had no caring model to emulate and when she was frustrated by her 'mothering' role, she also beat the hell out of us. When she became interested in boys, she brought them home, pushing us little ones out of the house, locking the door behind us. We were only allowed in when the boys had gone or our parents were expected home. There was no discipline, no order, no predictable routines; we were left to our own devices and had a licence to roam.

I was happy only when I received positive attention from my mother . . . which happened so rarely that I can remember most of those occasions quite well. She was not violent but she had a harsh tongue and specialised in verbal abuse.

Sex was a taboo subject in our household. Dirty talk, 'rude' behaviour, references to genitals or nudity constituted a serious, punishable offence. And when mum thought that it was time that I knew something about sex, she threw a book at me entitled 'Where babies come from' and said, 'Read that'. I found the contents totally irrelevant.

My introduction to sex as an act (as distinct from a story book mystery) happened when I was twelve years old. I was a lonely, shy child and felt so happy when I found a boy who liked me. We were the same age and got on so well that, very soon, I was invited to his house for weekends.

I never met my friend's mother. His father was a policeman. My introduction to sex was when this man tucked me into bed and put his hand on my penis. I was lonely and confused but not concerned because the man stroked the most intimate parts of my body as if it was the most normal thing to do. The concern came later when his sexual attentions became hurtful . . . both physically and emotionally. No-one tucked us into bed at home and, in the early stages, I presumed that genital touching was something that happened in caring families. I was affection starved and loved the attention. Given that I had been involved in genital fondling with other boys for a couple of years, I accepted it as 'normal'. But then the abuse became violent and sadistic.

The policeman enjoyed tying me to the bed, fastening my arms to the posts. If I resisted, as I did in those early days, he held his police pistol to my forehead. When I was absolutely terrified and shaking, he anally raped me.

About four weeks after this sadistic sex began, he took me to the home of another senior police officer. The two men said that they were taking me out for a drive to meet some friends who would be nice to me. When we arrived there, I was used for sex. Thereafter, I was used to provide sex for thirty nine men on a regular basis. Sometimes, there were groups of men present and sometimes there were other boys of about my age. Sometimes we met at the policeman's house and sometimes at a client's. I did not know until I was about fifteen that these policemen were selling me as a child prostitute. They received a minimum of $200 per client per session for my services and they kept every cent of it. This only came to light when one of my 'clients' asked me how much I was paid for sex. I didn't understand what he was talking about because I was paid nothing. I only did what I was ordered to do because my longing for attention had, by now, been replaced by total, abject fear. There was absolutely nothing that I could do to stop what was happening and there was absolutely no-one to whom I could turn for help. I never complained to my friend because I was terrified of losing his friendship. For many years, he was my one and only mate.

When I eventually realised that what was happening was wrong, I also realised the dangerous position that I was in. Twenty of the men were married and many had children of their own. Many, by virtue of their positions in the community, were obligated to protect children from abuse. And when my abusers were judges, magistrates, lawyers and police officers, I knew that I had no chance of reporting or stopping them. Where could I hide from such powerful people? Who would believe me and help me? Certainly not the police or the courts!

I was trapped and to remind me of my entrapment, whenever I hinted that I was dissatisfied with my life, a gun was placed in my mouth or against my forehead and I was reminded that my life was worthless.

I continued to be sexually abused by the two police officers and their thirty-nine clients until I was seventeen years old. By that time, I was taking drugs to escape from the reality of my life. I was ashamed of being a prostitute and the fact that, for five years, I had not even realised what I had become.

At the age of seventeen I joined the defence forces to escape from my predicament. I imagined that the Army was a haven for macho men but, once again, I was wrong. Some servicemen sensed that I had been victimised and they made my life hell. During the few months that I was in the service, I had one homosexual encounter and I was twice raped. I began to realise that I'd gone 'from the frying pan into the fire' and had a nervous breakdown which resulted in my release. Interestingly, my parents failed to realise that I had a problem even when I was admitted into psychiatric care.

When I returned home, the policeman visited me on the pretext of being concerned about my health. I asked my parents to tell him that I was too unwell to be visited but they insisted that he would be 'upset' if they turned him away. After all, he had always been 'so good' to me and they wouldn't want to hurt his feelings. When the policeman was satisfied that I hadn't revealed his paedophile ring to psychiatrists, he set about coercing me to return to work for him.

It was during this second period of my life as a prostitute that I committed my first sexual offence against juveniles. One of the wealthy clients required me to have sex with two fifteen-year-old boys so that he could record this on video. Although both of the boys were prostitutes, I felt evil and tainted by this role reversal. It gave me no satisfaction whatsoever but I did it because I was terrified of the police officers who were there giving the directions. I never saw the videos and have often wondered where they are and who is watching them.

At this stage, it was becoming obvious that I was too old for the paedophiles and most of them had lost interest in me. Eventually, they told me that they no longer wanted me and, once again, I was reminded that I would be shot if I ever disclosed what had happened. I decided to move away but there was no real sense of escape and I lived a life of fear, constantly obsessed with hiding my identity and covering my tracks.

I had my first relationship with a girl when I was twenty-one. I cared for her a lot but, when it came to lovemaking, I had no idea what to do. She had to demonstrate what was involved in 'normal' sexual relationships. I was completely bewildered, terrified of rejection and desperately afraid of making a fool of myself. She was patient and loving but the experience was disastrous. Having spent most of my life providing deviant sex for men, I felt totally inadequate with girls. I didn't know how to give real love, even less how to accept it. And, to make matters worse, I was as uncomfortable with 'gay' men as I was with heterosexual women.

At this point in my life, I felt that there was nothing left to live for and I attempted suicide. When I was released from hospital, I rented a flat and tried to hide from the world. Shortly afterwards, I found myself becoming attached to a fourteen-year-old youth who came to live with me. He was very much like me in that he had also been tricked into selling himself for sex. We had a great deal in common and he met many of my emotional needs. I wanted love and to be loved and he happened to be there when my need was greatest. Eventually, I involved him in oral sex and fondling.

This went on for two days and then the boy left. Afterwards, I felt guilty, remorseful, evil and suicidal when I realised that I had done to this boy what I hated having done to me. On the Sunday, I went to church and told the minister about what I had done. After hearing my confession, he made an appointment to see me again the following day.

At about four o'clock in the afternoon, I met with the minister, another church worker and, to my surprise, the youth who had been my victim. The minister asked me to repeat my story of what had happened and I omitted nothing. The boy looked directly at me from time to time and confirmed what I was saying by nodding his head. I was then asked to wait outside the office while the two men and the youth discussed the issues. When I was invited to return, the boy left and the minister told me of their decision. He assured me that what I had told them would be kept confidential but I must repent and ask the Lord for forgiveness, which I did. Then, the youth was invited to join us. The minister then set out the rules for our future conduct: we must

- not have any further contact with each other;
- attend church every week; and
- attend Bible study classes regularly.

I kept my contract but I soon found that repentance and following the minister's rules did not provide the expected cure for what I now recognised as a serious problem. I realised that I was neither heterosexual nor homosexual and could not cope with the guilt relating to what I had become. I felt more lonely and isolated than ever.

Then, my victim broke the rules and made contact with me. He demanded payment for his silence and threatened that if I failed to meet his demands, he would report me to the authorities. I took the gamble that he was bluffing and refused to pay. Again, I assessed the situation incorrectly and he reported me to the police. With the benefit of hindsight, he did me a favour because it was only the reporting that brought me into contact with a therapist who understood my problems.

Looking back, I often wonder what would have happened if my case had appeared before the magistrate who had used me as a child prostitute. Would he have found that there was no case to answer? And what would have happened if the judge responsible for sentencing me had been the judge that I knew so well? Would he have given me a good behaviour bond? Or would he have forgotten his own predilection for young boys and pronounced that I had committed a heinous crime and should be given a harsh sentence to deter others?

I pleaded guilty to the charges. Dad couldn't handle any of it and stayed away from the court. Mum supports me, as mums always do. In common with many other prisoners' families, Dad drives Mum to see me but he never comes inside the jail.

I am now on a programme for sex offenders and am being helped to deal with the disturbances associated with my childhood, family life and sexual victimisation. With professional help, I am beginning to understand myself, what I did and why I did it. For the first time in my life, the future looks bright. I have met a loving girl who will wait for my release. I will need help to develop a meaningful married sexual relationship but I am blessed in that I love her and she loves me. And that makes me realise that life without love is worse than no life at all.

In time, I will probably be able to bury most of my past and I am confident that I will not re-offend. I am equally sure that, wherever I live, I shall always be looking over my shoulder and will never be able to escape from fear.

8

The greatest taboo of all

I am a child molester.

That is the most difficult statement that I have ever had to make. I only found the courage to make it after intensive counselling and support.

Why was it so difficult?

Because I'm a woman!

Women aren't supposed to molest children. Motherhood is asexual, associated with purity, self-sacrifice and the Virgin Mary. The sexual abuse of children by their mothers is incomprehensible and unbelievable even in this rapidly changing world.

Until comparatively recently, people thought that, to stay safe, children only had to avoid male strangers wearing dirty old raincoats. Child sexual abuse didn't present a threat to parents when it was perceived as involving that readily identifiable group of men. After all, we wouldn't mix with anyone of that description, would we? No-one like that lives in our street or visits our house or works in our schools. In recent years, the media has delivered the message that strangers are not the greatest danger to children and that most child victims are abused by people they (and often their parents) know and trust. That message is much more difficult for adults to handle because it makes the world a less safe place and gives parents and teachers more responsibility for children's safety.

Anyone who has read articles or seen TV documentaries about child sexual abuse will have picked up the message that men are the main perpetrators and girls are almost always the victims. This message predominates in American child protection literature usually written by women social workers for parents and teachers to use with children. Offenders are consistently referred to as 'he' and potential victims as 'she'. This focus ensures that neither parents, teachers nor child protection workers expect to encounter male victims or female offenders. We seldom see what we don't expect to find and it isn't really surprising that the signs of abuse by women are often overlooked. Throughout the English-speaking world, the women's movement was at the forefront of publicising the abuse of female children by men. Women pioneered the establishment of Rape Crisis Centres and shelters to protect women and children from male violence. They gave other women the courage to reveal childhood abuse which they had previously kept secret. In the meantime, there was no similar recognition by male society of the existence and needs of abused boys.

Until comparatively recently, international statistics showed that only about 2 per cent of *reported* offences involved women perpetrators. Society had no problems with that kind of statistic because the 2 per cent were invariably the ones who acted under the control of men. That was reassuring because it told us that men were the ones responsible for child abuse and the female offenders were also their victims.

Sydney University Social Work lecturer Renee Koonin told the March 1994 Australian National Child Abuse Conference in Melbourne that women perpetrated between 14 per cent and 27 per cent of the abuse of boys and up to 10 per cent of the abuse of girls. The largest number of female offenders noted in the literature is in a study of college men by Fromoth and Burkhart (1988) in which 70 per cent reported that they had been sexually abused by women.

Koonin categorised women offenders into three groups:

- those who claim to love or 'want to teach' prepubescent boys about sex;
- those who are coerced by and act under the control of men; and
- 'predisposed offenders who have been sexually abused themselves'.

Koonin confirmed the reluctance of women to accept that solo female abusers exist because 'the women do it too argument can be used (by men) to deny the central importance of the abuse of male power in sexual abuse'.

Koonin noted that the very reluctance of women to accept that women offend ensures that their female victims 'have felt doubly silenced'.

Interestingly, when data from the Perth (Western Australia) male-survivor phone-in (1993) showed that more than a third of callers reported sexual abuse by females, some of the female organisers rejected the information and sought alternative explanations to account for the results. The explanation which best fitted their own ideology was that the calls were a 'hoax' perpetrated by paedophiles to implicate women and diminish the seriousness of their own offences. Interestingly, the professionals who took the calls were convinced of their authenticity.

The gap between the number of reports of female instigated abuse and the incidence reported by adult survivors should lead us to question why such a gap exists. My own experience suggests that it is a reflection of the denial of harm inflicted by females. Cases of abuse involving women are clearly under-reported but I also have reason to believe that the size of the problem is masked by the refusal of statutory authorities to take allegations of female–child abuse seriously. In particular, they tend to ignore mother–child incest which women can conceal in their day-to-day care-giving tasks. As a consequence, offences by mothers remain the world's best kept secret. Furthermore, women offenders are the ones least likely to be taken seriously when they seek help.

In recent years, enlightened health authorities have introduced offender treatment programmes (of various kinds and with various nomenclatures) to provide services in major cities. They tend to cater for convicted male sex offenders on parole as well as self-referred child molesters. But when I enquired about provision for women offenders, there was none. Staff at a State-funded centre freely admitted that they had no experience of working with women. And when, in desperation, I agreed to join an all-male group, I found that while I had a great deal in common with the male clients, the staff could not adjust their own entrenched sexist attitudes to cater for a female offender. They continued to refer to offenders as 'he' and victims as 'she', attributing child sexual abuse to the abuse of male power which, in my case, was blatantly inappropriate.

Tired of challenging them and sensing total despair, I found the courage to walk into the local police station where I asked to be arrested for molesting my children. When the youthful constable stopped laughing and realised that I was both sober and serious, he sent for the duty sergeant who declared that he had 'never heard of anything quite like it' in the whole of his police service and he hadn't the faintest idea what to do with me.

'Madam, I can't arrest you when there is no complainant,' he said, chewing the end of his pencil in a search for inspiration. 'Look! I've got it! Why don't you go home and make an appointment to talk it over with your family doctor.' With that, he bundled me out of his office, well satisfied that yet another problem had been resolved. I was not reported to the State child protection services by police or my general practitioner or by the psychiatrist to whom I was subsequently referred. No-one took a statement from me or interviewed my children. So much for child protection!

Throughout Western society, child sexual abuse is regarded as one of the most abhorrent crimes. The parent who commits incest violates the most sacred trust and the strongest of all societal taboos. Most people cannot begin to imagine how a parent can use a child for sexual gratification. This makes it very much harder for offenders to acknowledge that they have a problem. Women offenders are particularly handicapped by the convenient myths surrounding motherhood, such as that mothers have an innate capacity to nurture and protect children and that, by the very nature of things, motherhood is asexual.

With this kind of conditioning, it is inconceivable to most women that others might be sexually attracted to their children . . . least of all to young children. Female abusers know that, so far as female society is concerned, their offences amount to nothing less than sacrilege, if not high treason. Women who wish to confess are likely to find that nobody other than the parish priest wants to hear their confession (and I can confirm that an assurance that God has forgiven you is not the cure-all that it purports to be).

Why is it so difficult to understand female-initiated child sexual abuse? Long ago, researchers estimated that at least a quarter of male child victims become adult molesters. In other words, boys learn abuse, are damaged by it and repeat it. Given the statistical evidence that girls are at greater risk of victimisation than boys, why has it been so difficult for the experts to accept that some female victims are damaged in exactly the same way as male victims and some will inevitably repeat what they learned with younger children? Is the problem ignored because people think that abuse by women is less damaging (and therefore less important) than abuse by men? Is it because we perceive the penis as *the* dangerous weapon and, without one, the female offender must, of necessity, be less harmful? Do we regard abuse by women less seriously

140

because offenders cannot make their victims pregnant? Or are we influenced by long-standing male cultural attitudes which accept and even promote the idea that sex with older women is the ultimate beneficial educational experience for boys . . . the experience that 'turns boys into men'?

Is it the perceived harmlessness of abuse by females that prevents police and social welfare services from investigating and taking allegations seriously? Is that why children are left in the care of their mothers when maternal abuse has been disclosed? If so, I hope that my story goes some way to changing attitudes.

I was reared in a circus. No, it wasn't the kind of circus that performs in a Big Top in the park; our circus was a private family affair which had daily performances in our own home. In common with other family circuses, the children were trained from infancy to play their part. But unlike the circuses that you've seen, ours was a sex circus and my mother was the ring mistress. My older brother and I were the star performers. My mother, in true circus fashion, used a whip to make her performers engage in the gross acts that they often tried to resist.

My father is a lawyer and my mother a university lecturer whose work involves preparing students for careers noted for the provision of 'tender loving care'. They are both highly respected in the community. My father is a devout church worker and my mother is on all the 'do-gooder committees' which focus on protecting other people's children. The problem is, of course, that the more important the offenders and the more they are respected and trusted, the less likely that they will be suspected of sexual deviance, the less likely that children's allegations will be believed and the less likely that authorities will take action to protect victims. And that I learned the hard way.

I have blocked out and can remember very little about my pre-school years. At the age of five, I attended a co-educational fee-paying school in the capable hands of Sister Theresa. We lived in a large house with a huge garden and a heated swimming pool. We also had a house at the beach. I adored my father but he spent comparatively little time with us because of his work.

My induction to the sexual circus began in infancy but I went through the full initiation process when I was six. My mother decided that it was time for me to provide entertainment for my older brother who was then about twelve years old. She assisted him to rape me and when they found that physically impossible, he held me down while she enlarged my vaginal opening. I kicked and screamed and suffered enormous pain but received neither sympathy nor first aid from either of them. I was in agony long after this happened. It hurt when I sat down, it hurt when I walked but the pain was unbearable when I went to the toilet and urine splashed on the tear. I made excuses for avoiding physical education but the teacher insisted that I strip down to my pants to join others on the climbing apparatus. I protested that I didn't feel well and the teacher only took me seriously when the exercise opened up the wound and she saw blood on my pants. She expressed surprise then blushed with embarrassment. I hoped that she would ask me what had happened but she didn't. I suspect that this naive woman assumed that I had reached puberty somewhat prematurely and, with a hint of sympathy, she told me to return to the classroom, get dressed and rest. I hoped that the teacher would talk to my mother but nothing happened and the matter was never mentioned again.

Thereafter, when I arrived home from school, the circus performances were repeated. After a few months, my sister was also subjected to the same treatment and the circus acts expanded to include contortionist tricks and sexual acrobatics involving our German Shepherd dog. Sometimes, my mother had sexual intercourse with my brother and sometimes she held us down for him. She often raped us with objects which I prefer not to describe. When she became bored with one activity, she thought up another that was even more deviant and more painful than the last.

I sensed that there was something seriously wrong with our family because, apart from the pain that my sister and I suffered (which was supposed to be 'fun'), we were receiving conflicting messages. When we protested that we didn't want to play these horrible games, my mother assured us that what was happening was alright and 'it happens in all families'. She told us that our uncles and aunts did it with my cousins and my grandparents had done it with her. At the same time, we were told that we must keep the activities secret and she would kill us if we told anyone.

Before long, my brother began to abuse us without the help of my mother. We dawdled when we came home from school and he was often waiting to 'get' us when we arrived home. His demands became more and more sadistic but there was no-one to turn to for help. Our mother always protected him and referred to us as stupid, whingeing bitches.

It would have been good if I could have felt safe at school but I didn't; I was a total misfit from the very beginning. Worrying about what had happened the night before or what might happen when I returned home, I had no inclination to sit still on the classroom floor listening to the teacher's silly stories about billygoats and red hens. I couldn't concentrate for long enough to learn how to read and write and I soon became the class nuisance who was targeted for derision. And of course, children like to please their teacher and, whenever the opportunity occurred, they ganged up against me, knowing that they could rely on her support.

My mother always discouraged visitors and, as a result, my sister and I had no friends and we both found it difficult to relate to our classmates. We tended to seek each other's company in the school playground because other girls told us daily that they didn't want to sit by us or play with us. I had no idea how to make myself more attractive to them. To avoid complete social isolation, I set out to woo the boys. Wholly reliant on my knowledge of my brother, I took it for granted that the way to the hearts of five and six-year-old males was via their genitals. I shared a table with three boys and when I attacked their pants, they laughed and giggled and invited me to do it again. This provided a terrific boost to my self-esteem and eventually I decided to extend my circle of friends by tunnelling under the tables to tickle other boys in their sensitive places. They thought that this was great fun and, as no-one objected, I went on to explore the pants of every boy in the class. As my confidence increased I became more daring, targeting boys on the cushions in the reading corner and in the play house when the teacher's attention was elsewhere.

At some point, it occurred to me that I might be more popular with the girls if I included them in this game. I decided to focus on the child who rejected me most frequently. That was a big mistake because, no sooner had my hand strayed up her leg than she called out to the teacher for help. The teacher grabbed me by the collar, lifted me onto a chair and humiliated me in front of the whole class. I was presented as a dirty-minded brat whose disgusting habits made me unworthy of membership of this wonderful class in this wonderful school. ('And what would your mummy and daddy say if they knew what you did?')

The teacher invited the children to suggest suitable forms of punishment. The boys lapsed into fits of giggles while the girls suggested tortures befitting the novels of Edgar Allen Poe. The final indignity was being sent to the girls' toilets where, under supervision, I had to spend half an hour scrubbing my hands with disinfectant and a pumice stone until my fingers were red raw. My name went on the blackboard for bad behaviour and I was deprived of access to the playground for a week. I hoped that someone might ask me who had taught me to play these games but no-one did.

The compulsion to touch genitals continued but, thereafter, I restricted my attentions to boys and took more care not to get caught.

The abuse continued at home and, to cope with this, I learned to switch myself off so that my mind detached itself from my body and I became part of the ceiling. And there I stayed until it was all over. By that means, my body was used for sex but my mind remained free.

Matters came to a head at school when the teacher on playground duty caught me with my pants down exhibiting my genitals to a group of curious boys behind the bicycle shed. The teacher picked me up in the air, threw me over her shoulder and smacked my bare buttocks in front of the whole school.

Sister Teresa sent for my mother. I have clear recollections of standing in front of her desk which was so big that I could scarcely see over the top of it. She stressed how embarrassed she felt at being called to perform this painful duty but she could no longer conceal the complaints made by parents and staff about my immoral behaviour. She said that I was totally obsessed with sex, drew sexually explicit pictures, talked obsessively about genitals and excretion, had been reported for genital touching and now, in this latest incident, I had indecently exposed myself to boys. In a nutshell, I was perceived as a dangerous influence on other children and did not fit into this nice Christian fee-paying school. The teachers found my behaviour repulsive and, although they were bewildered why such a promiscuous child could have emerged from such a charming family ('and we really sympathise with you and your husband in these difficult circumstances') it would clearly be best for all concerned if other arrangements were made for me. I went down in history as being the youngest child to be expelled from that school.

If my mother was surprised by these revelations, she did not show it. She agreed that I was a problem child and suggested that the cause might lie in the fact that I was adopted. She explained that my mother was a university student whose immorality and irresponsibility had resulted in my birth and abandonment for adoption. 'Coming from a promiscuous mother, it's probably in her genes,' my mother said.

I had no idea what promiscuous meant and interpreted genes

as clothing but I memorised the conversation and asked my brother for a translation when I returned home.

My mother told Sister Teresa that she had 'tried for another child' after the birth of her son and, when nothing happened, she and Dad decided to 'go for adoption'. Almost as soon as I arrived, my adoptive mother found that she was pregnant, hence the narrow age gap between my sister and myself. The demeanour of the headmistress instantly changed. She assured my mother that she would be rewarded in heaven for taking such a difficult, unlovable child into her loving family. She hinted that my mother should segregate me from her other offspring because of the risk that I might contaminate them with my innate wickedness.

I was angry that I had learned in this way that this was not my real family. I didn't ask them to adopt me. I didn't want to be adopted by them. And while I accepted that my own mother had rights of ownership and could do whatever she wanted to me, I was convinced that adoptive parents did not have those rights. Thereafter, I refused to participate in their sexual activities and made it clear that I hated them and didn't have to obey their instructions. I was as provocative and as defiant as I could possibly be and spent a great deal of my time in tears. 'I don't have to do what you say, you're not my real mother', was my favourite cry and it was worth the punishment that inevitably followed. The circus continued however and my resistance merely increased the level of violence.

I was transferred to another private school of a different religious persuasion but nothing else changed. Isolated and lacking a normal home life, I still found it difficult to relate to my peers. I desperately wanted to be liked but I managed to destroy every budding relationship by being over-possessive and sexual. I trusted no-one and felt that I had to be in complete control; I demanded unconditional guarantees that these six and seven year olds would be my friends and mine alone (for ever and ever) and, of course, no-one needed to make or keep such promises.

As I grew older, I was rejected by both boys and girls. Initially, they were confused and sometimes curious about my obsession with genital fondling but eventually, they grew bored with it and taunted me. I fought back and often won by scratching and pulling hair for which I was publicly smacked by the staff.

When I was about twelve years old, my mother nagged my father to join in the family circus. Until then, he had been an observer and I sensed that he didn't really like what was happening but he was afraid of her. Gradually his involvement increased until he was using both my sister and I for sexual intercourse. I felt some sympathy for him because he was not cruel like my mother. He resisted her demands initially and he was always very apologetic both before and after sex. He usually gave me a Mars bar and said, 'I'm sorry if I hurt you'.

This was the only consideration that I experienced in my home life and I was touched by the hint of conscience. As a result, I kept a 'soft spot' for my father and viewed him more as a fellow victim than as an offender. It took my counsellor a considerable amount of time to convince me that my sympathy was misplaced and that my father was not a child but an adult who had a responsibility to protect me.

Secondary school was very much more troublesome than primary school. My sister had, by now, revealed to the world that I was a discarded, unwanted, adopted bastard and this information was often used against me. Only one thing made secondary school tolerable and that was the ease with which I could play truant between classes. Once the register had been taken, I could escape to freedom and no-one seemed to notice that I'd gone. When my sister discovered my secret, she blackmailed me into letting her come with me and we headed for the amusement arcades and the sleazy cafes where other truants congregated.

This was a whole new and exciting world of teen rebellion and when we were given the opportunity to try marijuana and sea sickness pills, we accepted them gratefully. In the meantime, we presented the outward appearance of a good practising Christian family. We went to church every Sunday, said our prayers and confessed our sins.

I was twelve when I was expelled from school for the second time. By now, I had discovered that alcohol helped to dull my senses and the world became more tolerable after two or more drinks. Sometimes, my sister and I got drunk on our way to school and giggled or slept throughout the morning lessons. The balloon burst when we were found semi-conscious in the girls' toilets when we should have been at religious instruction. Once again, I was expelled and, on this occasion, we were transferred to the State school where I was labelled as an emotionally-disturbed delinquent. A social worker was given the task of sorting me out. He was a caring sort of bloke but, of course, it never occurred to him that I lived in an abusive family and throughout the many hours I spent in counselling, he never asked the right questions.

Changes of school did nothing to change my sexual obsessiveness or improve my social relationships. I was always getting into trouble and did my best to shock the staff. The school principal sent for my parents when, on April Fool's Day, my sister and I got stoned, climbed onto the school roof and attached our clothes to the lightning conductor so that it looked like a pennant on a yacht. The principal used a loud hailer to order us to come down. She looked and sounded very silly so we sat in the gutter and threatened to jump off the roof. Someone sent for the police and the fire brigade and that was very entertaining . . . for a while.

My mother never told my father about what happened. She came to the school alone, making the excuse that he was working away from home. I remember the conversation well. The principal was overwhelmingly sympathetic towards my mother. Like her predecessors, she found it difficult to understand how such a charming family could have produced not one but two delinquent children. I was clearly labelled as the bad influence, first because I was marginally older than my sister but, more importantly, because I was adopted.

My mother smiled graciously and thanked the staff for their patience. She said that if they were worried about us in the future, they were to contact her and she would collect us immediately. With that, she took us home, whipped us and sent us to bed without supper.

I was introduced to hard drugs shortly afterwards and, of course, the only way that I could pay for them was by stealing money from home. My mother found out when, while I was off my face, I threw myself from a multi-storey car park, ending up in the intensive care unit of the local hospital. My mother knew the staff and, after they had pumped the chemical concoction out of my stomach, they allowed me to return straight home (without the customary interview with a hospital psychiatrist) on my mother's assurance that she could handle me.

At about this time, I began to make threats that I would report my parents' sexual activities to social workers. It was a brave thing to do given that this was the only family I had and I hadn't yet worked out whether having a bad family was better than having no family at all. My action was also foolhardy because it alerted my parents to the fact that I was now a danger to them. My mother made the first move and contacted social services. She told them that I was uncontrollable and that I slept around with boys, stayed out all night, was addicted to drugs and alcohol and stole money to pay for them. My school record confirmed her complaint. I was deemed to be 'beyond control' and was placed in a closed residential unit run by State social welfare services. It catered for adolescent males who had convictions for theft and violence (including rape), and girls, all of whom were victims of incest who had turned to drugs. There were two female social workers on day shift and male security staff were responsible for us from about five o'clock onwards. The night shift men had previously worked in the prison service with male prisoners and their attitudes towards female residents reflected their history. They often referred to us as whores, bags and sluts and when we protested about their language, we were told quite explicitly that 'What you need is a good fuck' and we shouldn't complain because 'You'll all end up as prostitutes'.

The building was not air-conditioned and, on hot nights, we slept on top of the sheets. The staff were expected to patrol our rooms at regular intervals and it was not unusual for girls to complain that they were disturbed in the night by male staff 'having a perv'. A female social worker was raped by one of the youths while the others watched. There was no empathy and she went on sick leave and never returned.

When I woke up to find the night shift worker on my bed, I reported it to the women social workers on day shift and they, in turn, informed the departmental manager. The women argued that the department had a responsibility to protect us and that it was irresponsible to house adolescent male sex offenders together with female sexual abuse victims and use male ex-prison officers to supervise them during the night. We learned that the manager dismissed their concerns as female hysteria, the female social workers were transferred elsewhere and the organisation of the establishment remained the same. The night shift workers accused us of concocting vicious lies to try to get rid of the staff we least liked and their unprofessional behaviour continued.

Occasionally, if I conformed to everyone's expectations and stayed out of trouble, I was allowed to go home for the weekend. On one of these occasions, I went to the city, met a group of people I knew in a cafe and returned home just before midnight. My mother must have heard me struggling to turn the key in the lock because she was standing in the hall waiting for me. She was in a rage because I had stayed out late and she hit me across the head, accusing me of being a prostitute. I suddenly realised that I was now both taller and stronger than her; I accused her of being a hypocrite and hit her back. I had wanted to do that for years. She fell backwards and cut her head on the corner of the hall table.

Blood ran down her face and, without asking any questions, my brother sent for the police and instructed them to return me to the centre.

I became very depressed and convinced myself that life wasn't worth living, that I had no future and everyone would be much better off if I killed myself. I became obsessed with death and, when the opportunity arose, I locked myself in the bathroom and slashed my wrists with a kitchen knife. My parents merely regarded this as a further example of my delinquent, attention-seeking behaviour which they attributed to my adopted status. The staff at the centre assured me that it was my life and if I wanted to kill myself, that was my prerogative 'but please don't make a mess in the bathroom for someone else to clean up'.

I was taken to the hospital to have my arms stitched and, while I was there, I slipped through a toilet window and escaped from my escort. Police found me sleeping in a concrete drain in the park. Staff at the centre refused to take me back and I was transported in a prison van to the women's prison. As I put on the new uniform, I couldn't help thinking that there was something wrong with a justice system which allowed someone who had not been charged with any offence to be incarcerated in a prison while those who raped me remained free.

One day, I was surprised to learn that I had a visitor. I was even more surprised to see that my visitor was Jim, the social worker from my secondary school. Jim said that he was sorry to learn of my predicament and he felt badly about it because he knew that he had failed me. He told me that my sister also had serious problems; she was on heroin, had overdosed and revealed the cause of our problems. Jim asked me whether I had been sexually abused by someone at home. This was the moment that I'd been waiting for and I told him everything. It was like vomiting after you've eaten bad seafood; you keep on and on until every little bit is out. And afterwards, I felt empty.

Jim spoke to the prison manager and she called the police. Two uniformed officers arrived and Jim outlined what he knew. I was taken to the police station where I was interviewed by two male detectives. They began to take my statement but stopped writing when I began to describe my mother's sexual activities.

'Come off it!' one said. 'You don't expect us to believe this garbage. I've met your parents. They wouldn't do that.'

The second detective agreed. 'If you think that a statement like this will get you off the hook from the mess you're in, forget it,' he said.

A woman police officer whispered that I could insist on having a medical examination if I thought that it would help but when I heard that the doctor engaged by police for this purpose was a man who played golf with my father, I declined the offer.

Jim was in the waiting room. He was aghast when he heard what had happened. He talked to my sister and found that she confirmed my story. They went to the police station together and, this time, the statement was taken down in full.

The next day, Jim was instructed to appear before the school principal. He was told that investigating child abuse cases was not his responsibility, that he had acted unprofessionally and must never contact me or my sister again. He was transferred to another city and, at the end of the year, his contract was terminated. A short time later, I was informed that police did not intend to prosecute my parents or my brother because my sister had retracted her statement and was receiving psychiatric treatment. I received a card on which she had written two words, 'I'm sorry'.

In the meantime, Jim received death threats, his office was broken into and his files relating to my sister and I were stolen. I was in no doubt that my mother and brother were jointly responsible for this harassment and I feared that they were capable of carrying out their threats. I had a nervous breakdown and was admitted to psychiatric care.

I married the first kind man who wanted to look after me, became pregnant immediately and gave birth to twin boys nine months later. The marriage was doomed to fail because I could never respond to his love-making; when I suspected that he wanted sex, I detached my mind from my body and moved up to the ceiling until it was all over. My husband did not understand and became impatient with my lack of responsiveness. He also wanted me to have the pregnancy terminated given my history of instability and lack of sound parenting models. I wanted a child to love and a child who would love me. I went to talk to counsellors who convinced me that I should let the pregnancy continue. I knew that there were risks involved but the one risk that I never bargained for was that I would become my children's molester.

My husband left me when the babies were a week old. If I could cope with twins, he clearly couldn't. I was already depressed as a result of the births and when I realised that I was alone and had two little boys dependent on me, I went into a state of grief.

I relied on my sons to meet my emotional needs and, seeking their approval, I found myself returning to my childhood obsession with genitals. Eventually, I phoned an incest survivor's support group. Although such groups do not normally cater for offenders, I was lucky enough to find a counsellor who was neither shocked nor surprised by my disclosure; she had heard many similar stories before.

Despite everything that happened to me in childhood, I knew very little about the dynamics and nature of child sexual abuse. From the age of six, I had been led to believe that I was the one who was different and that my vices were inherited from my evil mother. Although I had been subjected to every possible form of abuse, my adoptive parents presented themselves as my victims. They had, after all, taken me into their home and hearts and I was the one who let them down.

My children were placed in a good foster home where they are as safe as children can be. I see them regularly. I am learning the 'why' of my behaviour and methods of controlling it. And in the meantime, with support, I returned to school, got my life together and am now a second year social work student at university.

To date, we have had one lecture which mentioned child sexual abuse. The lecturer referred to offenders as men and victims as girls. I didn't challenge her. I couldn't without revealing what had happened to me. And would anyone have believed me? I don't think so. Do you?

9

One law for the rich and another for the rest of us

My mother knows that my father is a child molester. His second wife knows it too; she was there when he molested me. Even the police know what he is and what he did; they were told not once but several times. And yet he wasn't even interviewed, least of all arrested and charged with an offence. Why?

The only possible explanation that I can think of is that there is one law for the rich and another for the rest of us.

Unlike some of the contributors to this book, I did not fall into the category of the poor, unwanted or materially disadvantaged child; to the contrary, my father was (and probably always will be) wealthy and my parents fought a bitter court battle over the custody of their sons. Why my father wanted to retain control of us is open to debate and I suspect that he merely regarded us as possessions over which he had the rights of ownership. During my childhood, my father was one of the most powerful men in Australia. Although unhappy and unsociable, he had the magic touch in his business life. I was probably the only person in the world who hoped that the collapse of the stock market would leave him bankrupt. But he's still there . . . as arrogant and as untouchable as ever.

Unlike the other contributors to this book, I cannot escape from the perpetrator of my abuse. He appears (uninvited) in my home via the television screen. Sometimes, I open a newspaper and find his face staring at me. Would the world be so eager to rub shoulders with him, I wonder, if they knew him as I know him? Or is power and money and male mateship more important than morality?

I suspect that the answer is 'Yes' to both questions. But let's go back to the beginning.

I was introduced to sex by my older brother when I was about five years old. I did not regard it as unpleasant and, lacking information to the contrary, thought that it was normal bedtime and bath-time play. Although sibling incest continued throughout my childhood and adolescence, until my brother became an adult and left home, he gave no indication that he was being sexually abused by my father and that what he was doing with me was a re-enactment of that abuse.

My problems really began in earnest with the separation of my parents. It is worth mentioning that my mother left my father because she learned that he was molesting my brother who was about four years old at the time. I knew nothing about it until, as an adult, I revealed my own abuse. My father fought a bitter battle with my mother in the settlement after separation. He retained access to his sons on condition that another adult was always present in his company. That, of course, was a ridiculous, unenforceable arrangement because it is impossible to supervise children when they stay with their non-custodial parent for days and weeks at a time. My mother knew that she was powerless and told herself that her boys needed to know their father, irrespective of how she felt about him. She seems to have accepted my father's explanation that he was homosexual and that homosexuals do not molest children. He also seems to have convinced her that if any misbehaviour had occurred, it would not happen again.

When the marriage broke down, my mother had to return to her career to support us and we moved to another city. Life was comparatively frugal because, although my father was extremely wealthy, he has never been known for his generosity.

When we returned home from access visits, my brother and I were invariably unmanageable. We exhibited such emotionally-disturbed behaviours that my despairing mother eventually took us to see a well-known child psychologist employed by the child health service. The psychologist attributed our problems to the fact that we were missing and needed the 'firm hand and discipline of a father'. He advised my mother to transfer custody of her sons to her former husband as quickly as possible. She thought about it long and hard before she decided to follow the psychologist's advice. She rationalised that she was not coping well with us on her own. A devout Christian, she felt guilty about the divorce and the fact that it had left her children living in comparative

153

impoverishment in a small city cottage with a tiny back garden when we were accustomed to fresh air and the freedom of a rambling country property.

With no-one to support her, my mother believed that she had nothing to offer us except herself while my father was capable of providing for all our needs, including the best private school education.

Unbeknown to my mother, my father was already making a unique contribution to our education. He was not teaching us about the birds and the bees, reproduction and childbirth; he was showing us what incestuous fathers do to their sons and what bisexual men do to each other. That, of course, was why we were fractious and unmanageable when we returned home after our visits, why we clung to our mother, had night fears and wet our beds. Nobody understood the real cause of our problems because no-one asked the right questions.

I was introduced to homosexual sex at a very early age. My father was obsessed with it: sex talk, sexual touching, masturbation, homosexual pornography, group sex with male workers on his property. I was there. I was with him. I was watching, participating, constantly assured by my father that, 'Come on, this is fun. It's only sex. What's wrong with you? Look, everybody does it.' And he was right about that! In my father's circle, everyone seemed to be doing it. Groups of men masturbated each other while watching porn on the video in my house. And whenever we went out together in the Land Rover, my father expected to masturbate and be masturbated, even while he was driving the vehicle. I didn't want it . . . in fact I hated it, but when I objected, he indicated that I was abnormal. Paradoxically, I was left in no doubt that this is what real macho men did to each other and those who didn't join in were wimps.

As I grew older and realised that this didn't happen in other families, I longed for and pleaded with my father to be 'a real dad' who loved and cared for me as a person instead of using me for sex. My longing was in vain however. He didn't even understand what I was talking about.

The all-male group sex continued even when my father remarried. His new wife was a timid woman who obeyed his every wish. This included being the only female in the room when my father and his male sex partners watched hard-core homosexual porn and acted out what they saw. My stepmother was often present when my father abused me. The fact that she was there helped to confirm my father's assurances that what was happening was normal and fun and men do it with their mates all the time.

I never knew how my new stepmother felt about this because she always immersed herself in sewing or knitting which enabled her to distance herself from what was happening, lower her eyes and focus on her work. Did my father derive some perverted satisfaction from humiliating her in this way? Did he force her to watch what happened? If not, why did she tolerate it? Why did she never tell someone about what was happening to me? Was she dazzled by his wealth? What was the attraction that enabled her to remain with him in circumstances that most women would find intolerable? She appeared devoted to him in public but what she endured in private, no-one will ever know. There was certainly nothing attractive about her life. My father was not a sociable man and apart from his obsession with sex, his only other interest was in making money.

Although incest continued until I was eighteen, it never occurred to me that my father had, concurrently, abused my older brother. Throughout the years that we lived together, my brother was never present when my father used me for sex; we never talked about it because I assumed that it only happened to me. I thought that I was abused because I was different, that I deserved what happened because I was bad, unlovable and not worth loving as a 'real' son is loved. These were the only explanations that I could find for my father's behaviour towards me. And despite what he did, my father constantly berated me because I failed to match up to his definition of masculinity. I was a disappointment because I did not share his values. I did not care for violent team sports. I excelled at swimming because it involved no-one else and once my head was under water, I could escape from the world. I distrusted everyone and felt that I had to be self-reliant. I didn't want to be a billionaire, I wanted to be a social worker and help other people . . . a 'poofter's job' in my father's language.

Although I knew that he regarded me only as his sex object, I loved my father and desperately wanted to please him so that he would love me. This longing continued into adulthood and until recently, I could have forgiven everything if only he had said, 'I've been a rotten father. Please forgive me and give me another chance.'

I longed for that to happen. But, in the end, I had to accept that he didn't know what love was. Much worse, when I became independent and wanted to love others, I found that my own capacity for loving had been impaired.

155

Unable to create any meaningful relationship, I eventually returned to live with my mother. I obtained a place at university and, unmotivated and unable to concentrate on anything for any length of time, I deferred, changed courses and eventually dropped out. My father despised me for this failure because he was then at the peak of his success and expected his sons to follow in his footsteps.

My social and sexual relationships also presented problems. I found that I could only relate to girls who allowed me to control them. I only wanted violent sex and felt incapable of providing the love, respect and mutual sharing that was expected in heterosexual relationships. I tried the 'gay' world but that was helpful only to satisfy lust and, once again, I found that I was incapable of engaging in a mutually caring relationship. I wanted to be in control and I did not understand why.

I began to seek solace from my problems in alcohol abuse and, eventually, drugs. I drifted from place to place and job to job. My mother was frantic with anxiety but I could not share my troubles because I was convinced that I only had myself to blame for my damaged childhood.

Recognising that I had serious problems, I made an appointment to see a male psychologist. That took a great deal of effort because there is no community encouragement for male survivors of abuse to seek counselling and I had no idea where to go for help. I felt such an idiot when I began to tell my story. I could sense that the psychologist felt even more uncomfortable with me.

'Look,' he said (when I was only half way through my life history), 'this was all a long time ago . . . It's nearly three years since the last time it happened. Why don't you forget about it. Put the past behind you and get on with your life.' He left me in no doubt that, in a man's world, you either like sex or you reject it, but real men never complain about it, least of all several years later.

I sensed that my presence threatened this man's own sexuality. He didn't want to know that boys could be sexually abused; it was more comfortable to think that it didn't really happen.

So, I went home feeling more unhappy, helpless, hopeless, angry and more frustrated than before. Imagining that women would be more sensitive and more sympathetic, I decided to confide in my girlfriend. She was angry with me and did not disguise her contempt. 'You must have been stupid to have done that with your own father,' she pronounced. 'I think it's disgusting.'

No-one seemed to understand. No-one cared. No-one could be

trusted. I decided that I would have to keep my problems to myself and I drank more alcohol and popped more pills to avoid the feelings of despair.

The relationship with the girlfriend came to an end and others were of equally short duration. In the meantime, men identified me as a victim and I was raped not once but several times by strangers and men I knew and trusted. On one occasion, I accepted the invitation to have coffee with a well-known radio disc jockey in the lounge of an international hotel; my next recollection was waking up, partially dressed, in a hotel bedroom. I was alone and extremely sore. My fear that my drink had been 'spiked' was confirmed when I learned that my 'friend' had shared the room, left early, settled the bill and requested that I be left undisturbed. I didn't report this or other rapes because I assumed that I was the one who had the problem insomuch as I attracted this kind of attention.

I went from job to job with intermittent periods of unemployment. I was self-destructive in every aspect of my life. I knew that my mother worried about me. She didn't understand what was wrong with me and I felt badly about letting everyone down. And in the meantime my father seemed to go from success to success.

I was twenty-one when I learned that my brother had been admitted to hospital suffering from paralysis. The doctors were puzzled because they were unable to diagnose the cause. There was no sign of a viral infection and after batteries of tests, they realised that his problems were psychological in origin.

I was sitting by his bedside when the 'shit hit the fan' (as they say) and I suddenly realised what was wrong with my brother and what was wrong with me. A social worker told me of something that my brother had said which made no sense to her but made a great deal of sense to me. In his confused state, my brother used an expression which my father had often used with me . . . an expression reserved for those occasions when he used me for sex.

I suddenly realised that my brother had abused me throughout childhood because he was also being abused by my father. And throughout all those years, he too had kept this secret. The next day, I learned that Dad was about to visit my brother in hospital. I was outraged and found the courage to telephone him. I told him what I knew, pointing out that he was the cause of my brother's breakdown and the cause of my problems and if he came near either of us again, I would kill him. And I meant it!

He laughed, ignored my threat and came to the hospital. I alerted the doctors to the likely cause of my brother's illness and my father was banned from visiting him. He ranted and raved but, for once, no-one was afraid of him. That annoyed him because, of course, he was accustomed to getting his own way.

At that time, I had the first clear picture of the mess that my father had made of all our lives and I went into a state of grief. I was deeply shocked that he had abused my brother because I had always assumed that the problem was mine. I was disgusted by his behaviour with his sons and yet I felt guilty because sons are supposed to love their fathers, not hate them and want revenge. I went through periods of denial, depression, self-recrimination and self-hatred but most of all I mourned for the real father that I needed, never had and now had to accept that I would never have. Until that point in my life, I carried the lingering hope that we could, one day, develop a normal, caring father and son relationship. Now, I had to accept reality and abandon that dream and I was angry with my father for depriving me of what I perceived to be my birthright.

I decided that it was time to tell my mother about what had been happening for most of my life. She, of course, was shocked and felt guilty because, with the benefit of hindsight, she could recall the many signs that we had given that something was seriously amiss. She read a book on child sexual abuse and realised that, from early childhood, both my brother and I had exhibited all of the signs and symptoms of victimisation which she had mistakenly labelled as troublesome but normal stages of child development which would pass. Now, she felt so badly about it that I found it difficult to burden her with the detail of what happened.

Far from being contrite, when my father learned that his secret was out, he became vindictive. His first punishment was to deprive me of access to a small allowance from my grandparents. I found lawyers who were prepared to fight him and, eventually, he settled his debt. It was not a large sum of money and I must confess that the lawyers gained the lion's share of it and I spent some of it in ways that I knew would be anathema to my father. Although it was a case of 'cutting off my nose to spite my face', I gained some pleasure from that realisation.

It would have been helpful if I could have formed a close bond with my brother but, after discovering that I knew his secret, there was little communication between us. He clearly did not want to talk about what had happened and my efforts to persuade him were rejected.

I decided to 'go it alone' and, with the support of my mother,

I went to the police. On the first visit, the Detective Sergeant paid careful attention to my statement until he heard the name of the accused perpetrator.

'Do you mean *the* . . .'

'Yes.'

He paused momentarily then tore up the partially completed report form into tiny pieces. When he finally spoke, he said, 'Well, sir, it's like this. As these offences were committed in other States, there's nothing that we can do. You'll have to go to the police in the relevant States and report it to them.'

'But surely you could take a statement here and pass it on to them?' my mother responded.

'No, you'll have to go there and do it yourself,' the policeman said. I didn't believe it and nor did my mother, but we were escorted out of the office so quickly that there was no opportunity to argue.

Shaken but not deterred, we tried again. On the next occasion, we asked to speak to the regional Detective Inspector. He showed considerable interest until, once again, we gave him the name and address of the offender and then he laughed. It was a nervous kind of laugh. He realised that laughter was inappropriate and apologised. When he recovered composure, he said: 'Look son, you're over the age of eighteen . . . it's a case of consenting adults'.

'But he was six or seven when it started,' my mother said. 'He was too young to give consent.'

'Sorry, I can't help you,' the Inspector replied.

The more I was thwarted, the angrier and more determined I became. By now I loathed my father and what he represented. I wanted to humiliate him as he had humiliated me. I wanted to hurt him as he had hurt me. I fantasised about killing him but, of course, I had neither the temperament nor the means to carry it out. I was also conscious of the fact that my family had suffered enough without having a murderer on their hands.

Our next stop was the office of a social worker. She telephoned a CIB Superintendent and told him of my failed efforts to obtain police support. I could hear the other half of the conversation and noted that, again, he was interested until he learned who I was. On this occasion, he said, 'I'm afraid there is nothing that I can do to help you. There's a three year limit on reporting . . . and it's more than three years since the last offence was committed.'

I did a quick calculation and realised that the third anniversary of the last offence was still a month away. This was pointed out to the Superintendent.

'Listen to me,' the detective said at last. 'You're wasting your time. His father may be the biggest bastard on earth but he can afford to buy the whole bloody legal profession . . . QCs and all . . . Do you have any idea what his defence counsel would do to the lad in court? Does he know what he's letting himself in for? The lawyers would tear him to shreds. And even if he could cope with that, we'd never get a conviction. Would any jury believe that he would do that to his own kids? Not a chance! We would be wasting our time! And even if we got a conviction, a guy like that would appeal on some legal technicality which had nothing to do with the offences. He's the sort of person who could afford to buy adjournments for months or even years on end. It would be stressful for everybody but most of all for the victim. And what would he get out of it? Even if his father went to jail, which is very unlikely, his identity would not be revealed by the media because the court's primary concern is to protect the identity of the victim. You wouldn't get the satisfaction of seeing him humiliated publicly. So what's the point? Tell the boy to go home, put it behind him and get on with his life.'

I went home but I couldn't get on with my life and I couldn't forget it. My life was a mess and I was angry, not least because I had to accept that my father was still in full control and able to buy anything that he wanted . . . even immunity from the justice system.

When justice evaded me, I turned my attention to the media . . . first to talk-back radio and then a television programme on child protection issues involving a live audience. These efforts involved a great deal of emotional trauma but they were in vain; I was either dubbed out by the programme's editor or the interviewer ignored my presence. I talked to politicians of the same political persuasion as my father and even met newspaper journalists. Again, everyone was interested in what I had to say . . . until they realised who I was. Then they gave me the run-around, explaining that they would have to discuss this with their seniors and I heard no more.

Despite the efforts that my mother and I have made, the invitation to contribute this chapter was the first invitation that I have ever received to tell my story in its entirety. And even now, the perpetrator of the abuse, my father, is protected by both the editor and the publisher of this book to the extent that I am unable to use my own name and I have had to change or delete factual information which might possibly lead to his identification. Yes, even now, my father has all the rights and no-one dares to challenge him. And yet when I was a child, I had no rights and he failed to protect me.

Life is still very fragile. I have periods of depression and periods of resentment. I flit from place to place and job to job (to quote my mother), always searching but never quite sure what I am searching for. My family thinks it's time that I 'got my life together', settled down with a wife, a mortgage and children of my own. They cannot understand that I am afraid of marriage: in the last twenty years, I have witnessed many divorces in my immediate family circle and I am acutely aware of the lack of sound models to carry me through. I understand the responsibilities of parenting and realise that, with a long history of abuse, it would be dangerous to have children of my own.

Yes, I sometimes look at boys and find them sexually attractive. My eyes leave their faces and glance down at their bodies. This terrifies and disgusts me and I hate myself when it happens. These thoughts seem to stay in a corner of my mind and leap out when I least expect them.

My brother has consistently avoided facing up to what happened to us. Whenever we meet, we talk only about trivia. He has never given me permission to discuss the pain we have in common. We know that my father caused his illness but the detail of what he did is still his secret and he has been more successful than I in presenting an image of normality. I love him dearly and worry about him a great deal. He has married and now has children. The rest of the family think that this is wonderful and ask why I can't be more like him. I just worry about the children. Does his wife know the family history? Does she understand the risks involved? I doubt it! It is even feasible that, while playing at 'happy families', someone might suggest that grandpa should be given the chance to meet his grandsons.

In the meantime, I delved into my father's past to try to understand why he is what he is. I learned that he was pack-raped as a child by gangs of sheep shearers working on a relative's farm. My father was badly injured and his injuries necessitated hospitalisation. My grandparents thought that this was a family disgrace and my grandfather bribed the nurses to keep it secret. The matter was never discussed again and everyone tried to pretend that it didn't happen. Naively, they thought that if no-one talked about it, my father would also forget about it. We have all paid heavily for that secret.

I have given this a great deal of thought and know that the final straw that would tip me over the edge would be to find that either my brother or I had created the another generation of victims. My worst nightmare involves us going to jail. The thought of this chills me to the bone, even though the temperature is 30°C and the humidity is currently 80 per cent.

At an intellectual level, I know that sex with boys is wrong and I loathed what happened to me. I understand only too well how damaging it is. At the same time, I was taught that sex with boys is 'fun' and the lessons were given by my most influential teacher. That learning continued throughout my most formative years. I only hope and pray that both my brother and I have the strength to resist temptation. And although it may seem illogical to the reader, while wanting to see my father sent to jail, I feel that it would be terribly unfair if my brother or I were caught, convicted and given a prison sentence when our abuser was allowed to remain free of the law merely because he is rich. But then no-one ever promised that life would be fair, did they?

Postscript: Boys—
the forgotten victims

Freda Briggs

The problem of child sexual abuse was brought to the notice of the English-speaking world by the women's movement in the mid-1980s. Statistics relating to reported cases suggested that the problem was much greater for girls than for boys and, furthermore, that men were almost always the abusers. This trend was confirmed when international researchers surveyed university students and random samples of adults to enquire whether or not they had been sexually abused in childhood. Nobody realised that the men were being asked the wrong questions. And because findings consistently showed that female children were at greatest risk of abuse, support services were set up by pioneering women for female clients.

As supporting child protection issues was (and to some extent, still is) regarded by (predominantly male) politicians as akin to 'political suicide', it is not surprising to find that services were set up with considerable emphasis on voluntary help and minimal or no government funding. Some Rape Crisis Centres displayed notices on their doors which said, 'Men are not allowed beyond this point'. There was a tacit assumption that boys and men were either not raped or, alternatively, that the few who suffered should be acknowledged and supported by male society. With the author's knowledge, men who felt strongly about the lack of help for abused boys wrote letters to the national and local press and not a single letter was published.

Because women were at the forefront in publicising the size of the problem and its cost to individuals and the community, child molestation was commonly viewed as an issue for girls or, worse, a 'women's problem'. This view was sustained by those members of the judiciary who accepted the defence's explanation that the accused men were seduced by their five or six-year-old harlot daughters and were more to be pitied than blamed. Like adult rape victims throughout the ages, children were held responsible if they did not fight back, scream or complain immediately to the authorities—even when the perpetrator was their primary caregiver, twice their size and woke them up in the middle of the night. By disregarding the adult–child power differential and apportioning blame to victims, the justice system contributed to the myths surrounding child sexual abuse and made it harder for both child victims and adult survivors to reveal their experiences.

In the meantime, the only men who dared to voice an opinion on the subject were the professionals employed in child protection and those who, threatened by the growing number of reports and fearing false accusation, spread fear among family-minded people. Under the guise of defenders of the family as an institution, they gained a disproportionate amount of media attention, telling the world what people wanted to hear: that police statistics were misleading, that incest was not a problem and that the child protection movement was part of a sinister lesbian–feminist plot to destroy traditional society. The same men vociferously opposed the introduction of child protection programmes on the basis that they were designed to make children suspicious of their fathers and that they placed all men at risk of being accused of abuse. Opposition politicians (of all parties) listened to and supported their cause.

In this climate, few men dared to admit that they had been abused and those who did disclose their survivor status over a bottle of claret invariably added, 'I don't know what the fuss is all about. It happened to me and I'm alright', confirming that they were strong, brave and uncomplaining and female victims should be more like them.

Throughout most of this period, the protection of boys was ignored. No-one jumped up and down demanding services for male survivors of abuse and rape. No-one challenged international statistics which showed that, throughout the English-speaking world, girls reported abuse four times more frequently than boys. It was assumed that either boys were less vulnerable to sexual molestation or they were not damaged by it.

Even when it was realised that male victims are at high risk of becoming the next generation of sex offenders, the protection and treatment of boys received scant attention. There was no community encouragement for male victims to report offences and, worse, outside the USA there was no serious attempt to persuade offenders to seek help. Much worse, there was little or no help available and those who found the courage to seek it were often 'put down' by homophobic male psychologists who told them (in various ways) that they should have prevented the abuse or enjoyed it but they certainly should not complain about it. Mic Hunter, in his book *Abused Boys: The neglected victims of sexual abuse* (1990) confirms that men in North America experienced the same phenomenon when they sought counselling for rape or childhood sexual abuse.

In the mid-1990s, there is still a tendency for child protection representatives to persuade governments that money should not be wasted on programmes for offenders but should be allocated to services for victims. Certainly, services are inadequate and unless we provide better child protection education for professionals, parents and children, and better support and therapeutic services for victims and their non-offending family members, there will be more offenders committing offences in the future.

As the contributors to this book have clearly shown, child sexual abuse is learned and the most vulnerable children are those who lack information and affectionate, supportive parents. International researchers claim that, without helpful intervention, about a quarter of male child victims become offenders. The 'Don't spend money on those bastards' approach is clearly short-sighted given that an offender is capable of damaging hundreds of lives.

Child protection programmes do not cater for boys

In the 1970s, American social workers recognised the inappropriateness of 'dangerous stranger' information presented to school children and they replaced it with 'empowerment' programmes which told children that they had the right to be 'safe, strong and free'. One of the first of these was the Child Assault Prevention Project, known as CAPP. A more recent 'empowerment' programme, Protective Behaviours, was introduced to Australian education authorities in 1985.

With the benefit of hindsight, American researchers Finkelhor and Strapko (1987) noted that, while programmes were introduced with a great deal of enthusiasm and users made wide claims relating to their effectiveness, there was little or no research evidence to show their effectiveness or their appropriateness for children's developmental levels. CAPP and other American school programmes were adapted from the 'empowerment' models used by women social workers in Rape Crisis Centres with adult female clients. And although they were a great improvement on the ubiquitous 'dangerous stranger' message, they were constructed from the adult female's perspective of sexual abuse rather than the child's perspective. The designers made the following assumptions which were incorporated in their programmes:

- that the concepts used successfully with adults would be appropriate for male and female children of all ages;
- that child sexual abuse produces negative or unsafe feelings which children can learn to recognise and act upon;
- that sexual touching is unwanted and unpleasant and can be identified as 'yucky', bad or 'unsafe' touching which must be rejected and reported; and
- that children can be empowered to say 'No' to sexual touching, report it and continue reporting it until adults respond appropriately.

These assumptions were incorporated into child protection literature and kits which were released throughout the English-speaking world. As the contributors to this book have demonstrated, the designers were not meeting the needs of boys. (See publications by Abel *et al.*, Wyre and Bentovim.) Programmes failed to take account of the fact that boys:

- live in highly sexualised peer group environments;
- are handling their genitals on a daily basis and are not subjected to the same notions of body privacy and genital secrecy as girls;
- are sexually curious at an early age and paedophiles tap into that curiosity by introducing pornography and conversation about masturbation and oral sex before they introduce sexual touching;
- often find 'dirty talk' exciting, especially if they lack relevant sex education and their parents are perceived as unapproachable;
- sometimes view genital touching and oral sex as pleasurable and loving, especially in the early stages of the seduction process when they are the recipients of attention and no demands are made for reciprocation;
- blame themselves for the abuse, especially if they liked the attention which accompanied it; and
- sometimes go looking for sexual contact when they associate it with affection and approval.

Child protection education and services take no account of the fact that sexually-abusive behaviour is learned and children who are introduced to sex at an early age may become obsessed with it and introduce it to their peers. Victims are often caught abusing younger children in pre-school centres, classrooms and school toilets but, when staff are uninformed, they often mistake abusive activities for signs of early sexual development. 'They must have seen blue movies at home' is a common explanation for ignoring evidence of early sexualisation. The offences of many a juvenile perpetrator have been dismissed with laughter and the statement that, 'boys will be boys'. Other offenders are reprimanded. Their sexual behaviour continues but they 'take care not to get caught'. Unfortunately, if there is no helpful intervention, there is a high risk that juvenile perpetrators will become adult perpetrators.

Women offenders: the perpetrators we try to forget

In the 1980s, allegations of sexual offences involving women constituted between only 1–3 per cent of all reports throughout the Western world. At the 1991 European Conference on Child Abuse and Neglect, it was noted that reports of abuse by females had increased substantially in the preceding year. The same trend was noted in Australia. Since 1991, however, statistics relating to reports of abuse involving male victims or female offenders have become harder to find. In South Australia, the Department for Family and Community Services no longer records the gender of the offender or the gender of the victim for statistical purposes.

Society has ignored the existence of, and the psychological and sexual damage caused by, female offenders in much the same way as it has failed to recognise the risks to boys. Victims invariably feel that they were more damaged by the psychological aspects of the abuse than the sex. Marvasti (1986) points out that adult female offenders are 'usually non-violent and at times quite subtle'. They go undetected because most offences are incestuous and boys are unlikely to report their primary caregivers or older sisters, least of all if they are being abused by other relatives simultaneously, as often happens in incestuous families. As adults, survivors describe the accompanying psychological abuse as by far the most damaging aspect; the sexual component is seldom the greatest concern of male victims. Reports show that cases of mother–son incest are only likely to be disclosed in long-term therapeutic treatment and, even if reported, are seldom taken seriously by child protection authorities (Lawson 1993) .

Male victims don't always realise that they have been abused

The greatest deterrent to reporting is the fact that male victims seldom realise that what happened to them constituted abuse. If males enjoyed any aspect of the sexual behaviour or did not say 'No' or fight back, they seldom classify sex acts with adults as 'abuse' or 'unwanted sex'. If the act was non-violent or involved a female, they are even less likely to categorise it as 'abuse'.

Given that the male culture tells boys that sexual experiences with older women provide the ultimate educational experience, how can they tell anyone that they did not like it? Boys are taught that they must be self-sufficient, strong and brave and they know that an admission of victimisation is likely to be associated with character weakness or identification with homosexuality.

Researchers have also contributed to the myths relating to the incidence of sexual abuse among boys because the wrong people asked the wrong questions. With the stigma associated with homosexual abuse and the fact that most men have no opportunity to work through their feelings about what happened to them in childhood, male survivors are not usually willing to tell their secrets to male academics or young research assistants of either gender.

American researcher David Finkelhor (1986) found that men did not disclose their abuse in response to open-ended questions. Some said that they had not been abused (when they had) because their definition of abuse was often markedly different to the definition used by the researcher. In 1993, British researcher Kevin Browne told an Australasian Child Abuse Conference in Brisbane that, in a survey of convicted child molesters, only half reported that they had been sexually abused in childhood. When questioned by members of the audience, Browne revealed that he had had to abandon the interviews because the prisoners were uncomfortable with a young male academic. Research findings will vary markedly depending on the ability of the interviewers to make survivors feel at ease. The danger is that government agencies which are reluctant to spend money will be even less inclined to invest in offender programmes if academics are assuring them that child molesters offend just because they feel like it.

Adult males tend to reveal abuse accidentally after months of counselling for psychological, sexual and social problems. Unfortunately, as our study shows, sexual abuse is damaging irrespective of whether victims regard it as harmful or 'normal'. Even when men are in jail for repeating the behaviour inflicted upon them, they are rarely aware of the connection between their past learning and their present predicament. Interestingly, because boys accept responsibility for what happened to them and believe their abusers' explanations that they are either educating them about sex or demonstrating their love, male victims seldom have hostile feelings towards the abusers who wrecked their lives. Resentment is least likely when neither violence nor force were involved. They disregard the tricks, bribes and blackmail used in the seduction process and accept equal responsibility for their predicament, albeit at six or seven years of age. The exceptions are, of course, the men who were subjected to sadistic abuse at the hands of priests, Catholic Brothers and men employed as parent replacement figures by child welfare authorities.

The need for more appropriate sexuality education for boys

Although boys are given considerably more freedom than girls, their sexuality education has been neglected even more than the education of their sisters. This is probably due to the fact that boys do not menstruate or become pregnant and parents have not yet accepted the importance of teaching children to respect and take care of their genitals to avoid sexually transmitted diseases. Current parent education programmes also emphasise the importance of ignoring children's sexual curiosity and exploration with peers (to reduce the likelihood of guilt and secrecy) but, as we have seen in this study, obsession with exploration increases the vulnerability of boys to adult predators.

The contributors to this book also demonstrated in a very poignant way that the lack of sex education contributed to their abuse. Clearly, a little knowledge about the birds and the bees and 'where babies come from' will not satisfy boys' curiosity about their own bodies nor will it protect them from homosexual offences. Unless we provide information which children can understand, they will acquire inappropriate information from other people.

Although some parents and teachers will resist it, there is a clear need for developmentally-appropriate sexuality education to be taught side by side with education for child protection. This needs to be written by men with boys in mind. With no history of involvement, parents (and fathers in particular) will also need practical help on how to provide more effective protection and support.

If there is one message that comes out of this study, however, it is that boys need to receive approval and physical affection from their fathers. Of all the factors which contribute to the vulnerability of boys to sexual abuse, the lack of a warm, affectionate father figure appears to be the most significant factor of all.

References

Abel, G., Becker, J.V., Cunningham-Rathner, J.C., Rouleau, J.l. and Murphy, W.D. (1987), 'Self-reported sex crimes on non-incarcerated paraphiliacs', *Journal of Interpersonal Violence*, vol. 2, no. 1, pp. 3–25

Bentovim, A. (1991), 'Evaluation of a comprehensive treatment approach to child sexual abuse within the family', paper presented at *Third European Conference on Child Abuse and Neglect*, Prague, June 1991

Briggs, F., Hawkins, M. F. and Williams, M. (1994), 'A comparison of the childhood and family experiences of convicted, incarcerated male child molesters and men who were sexually abused in childhood and have not committed offences against children', Report to the Criminology Research Council, University of South Australia

Finkelhor, D. (1986), *A sourcebook on child sexual abuse*, Newbury Park, Sage

——(1979), *Sexually victimised children*, New York, Free Press

Finkelhor, D. and Strapko, N. (1987), *Sexual abuse prevention education: a review of evaluation studies*, University of New Hampshire, Durham, vs 54, prepared for Diana J. Willis, E. Wayne Holder and Mindy Rosenberg (eds), *Child Abuse Prevention*, New York, Wiley

Lawson, C. (1993), 'Mother–son sexual abuse: Rare or under-reported? A critique of the research', *Child Abuse and Neglect*, vol. 17, pp. 261–9

Marvasti, T. (1986), 'Incestuous mothers', *American Journal of Forensic Psychiatry*, vol. 7, no. 4, pp. 63–9

Wyre, R. (1987), *Working with sex abuse: Understanding sex offending*, Oxford, Perry Publications